TO
ACKNOWLEDGE
A
WAR

TO ACKNOWLEDGE A WAR

The Korean War in American Memory

Paul M. Edwards

Contributions in Military Studies, Number 193

GREENWOOD PRESS
Westport, Connecticut • London

*D S
9 1 8
. E 3 9
2 0 0 0*

Library of Congress Cataloging-in-Publication Data

Edwards, Paul M.
  To acknowledge a war : the Korean War in American memory / Paul M. Edwards.
    p. cm.—(Contributions in military studies, ISSN 0883–6884 ; no. 193)
  Includes bibliographical references and index.
  ISBN 0–313–31021–1 (alk. paper)
  1. Korean War, 1950–1953. I. Title. II. Series.
  DS918.E39   2000
  951.904′2—dc21   99–049887

British Library Cataloguing in Publication Data is available.

Library of Congress Catalog Card Number: 99–049887
ISBN: 0–313–31021–1
ISSN: 0883–6884

First published in 2000

Greenwood Press, 88 Post Road West, Westport, CT 06881
An imprint of Greenwood Publishing Group, Inc.
www.greenwood.com

Printed in the United States of America

The paper used in this book complies with the
Permanent Paper Standard issued by the National
Information Standards Organization (Z39.48–1984).

10 9 8 7 6 5 4 3 2 1

This book is respectfully dedicated to Mark F. McKiernan, Ph.D.

Contents

Acknowledgments

The essence of true research is to involve
the entire community.

Lewis Oglethorpe

Any research project reflects the contributions and abilities of many persons. This is particularly true for research about the Korean War. The materials about the war remain widely scattered. Many of the primary works necessary for completion of a narrative such as this are to be found in the monographs covering the subject. It is in locating these isolated works that I have sought the help of many people.

Because there are so many, and because the persons were often just doing their jobs in their normal efficient manner, I will not try to mention them all. Some, however, have gone out of their way to be of special help.

Of the many who went "beyond the call of duty" to be of assistance, I wish to acknowledge my deep appreciation to the librarian and the staff of the Combined Arms Research Library at the Command and Staff College, Fort Leavenworth, Kansas; the librarians of the Army History Center, Carlisle Barracks, Pennsylvania; the staff at the Air Library at Maxwell Air Force Base in Montgomery, Alabama; helpful persons at the Miller-Nichols Library of the University of Missouri (Kansas City); the librarian and staff of Park College in Parkville, Missouri; and the research library staff of the Kansas City Public Library and the Mid-Continent Library in Jackson County.

Special thanks must go to the board and the staff of the Center for the Study of the Korean War, located in Independence, Missouri. This unique collection of Korean War letters, diaries, orders, and photographs is the source of much of the primary material consulted.

It would irresponsible not to acknowledge the help of Tammy Lindle, who so graciously spent her time reading the manuscript and has helped in so many ways to make this book possible. To Lyman F. Edwards, North Kansas City, goes my appreciation for help and guidance throughout the process.

Several other persons have contributed in a variety of ways. I would like to acknowledge my gratitude to James Cadberry, historian; Tim Rives of the National Archives (Kansas City); Vice Chancellor Marilu Goodyear of the University of Kansas, in Lawrence; Adrian Alexander of the Big Twelve Library Consortiums; Frank Kelley of San Francisco, for so much; Beverly Spring of Independence, Missouri; Nancy Eisler of Graceland College; Sue MacDonald, librarian; Dr. Michael Pearlman of the Command and Staff College; my son Greggory M. Edwards, author and teacher; long time good friend and moral support Gregory Smith; and Laura Lane and Randy Hallauer, both of Baker University, Overland Park (Kansas), who contributed in their own special ways. Also, of course, my deep and continued appreciation goes to my wife, Carolynn Jean Edwards, keeper of the flame.

Chapter 1

Introduction

The war was a defining event in the long peace
between the Soviet Union and the United States.

William Stueck

War is about fighting, and killing, and dying. While the field of battle is often a place of heroes and honor, wars are not heroic nor do nations engaged in war act honorably. War is an aspect of human life that has been with us since men and women first decided to record their past, and probably long before. Fighting seems to be as much a part of the human condition as is love. Many feel that the condition of war is a natural state. There may be some truth in this idea. The difficulty in understanding war as phenomenon is compounded by the fact that while killing may be natural, it does not necessarily follow that war is. The desire to kill appears to be conditioned; is the willingness to kill more the product of rational consideration?

There is still considerable disagreement concerning the methods by which the figures of combat firing are collected. But there appears to be general agreement about what they suggest. S. L. A. Marshall provided most of these figures. During the fighting in World War II, only 15 percent to 20 percent of those on the line actually fired their weapons. In Korea, it is suggested that something like 45 percent of the infantry engaged actually shot their weapons with the intent to kill. But in Vietnam, the percentage of those firing their weapons rose to nearly 90 percent. Without jumping to too many conclusions, it does seem clear that the circumstances, the conditioning, or perhaps the natural reluctance to kill, has changed. More and more American men and women are willing to kill when in combat.

The jury is still out about which came first; violence and then conditioned behavior, or conditioned behavior and then violence. But one thing is clear. While the military has been fairly successful in conditioning young men and women to kill, they have made little or no effort–nor has anyone else–to recondition those who were taught to act on impulse rather than reason.

It is in part this conditioning to the act of killing, and the desire to control it, that has led so many veterans simply to withdraw, to put their experiences behind them. They just never talk about the depth of their involvement again. Likewise, it is rare for the military, or the government, to acknowledge the vast human costs of war. A large measure of this price is paid after the fact by the veterans involved. Despite the material costs, so well detailed, the psychiatric breakdown of the individual still remains one of the more costly effects of war.

THE PROCESS OF KILLING

The process of killing is usually associated with the midbrain. The midbrain in humans is very much like that of all other animals. It is, as well, that part of the human mind that behavior psychologists have determined can be influenced by conditioning. This conditioning is what basic training is all about. Basic training is designed to take impressionable young persons and teach them to act instinctively, to follow orders, and to override whatever natural tendencies they possess to flee rather than fight.

When persons get involved in controversy, when they are relentlessly attacked, they are inclined to "lose their reason." That is, a person's response moves from the forebrain, which acts from reason, to the midbrain, which acts by conditioning. The goal of civilization is to reverse this natural response, to make people less inclined to kill. Over the years, to some degree, this has worked. It does not always work, of course, but the effort has met with considerable success. The rational concerns of the civilized world have taught us to control the unreasonable act of killing. Yet, in contrast, we have just as willingly worked to condition some members of our society to kill, relying on the midbrain functions to overcome the restraint imposed by reason and civilization.

War is the response of persons who feel they have been pushed too far, who desire too much, or who feel dishonored. War is the response of persons and nations who are threatened and afraid. War is the response of persons who feel cheated. War is the assumed solution to injustice; it is the ultimate answer to the question of who is in charge. It is the pragmatic answer to the failure of other means of settling disagreements. War has caused uncounted death and destruction not only for armies and nations but also for millions of persons not even aware of what the wars were about.

What went on in Korea in the early 1950s was a war. It was a period of fighting and dying on a massive scale. The fact that it has been called a police action, or a conflict, an Asian civil war, an imperialist act, a bold act of containment, or a United Nations imperative, does not change what happened in Korea. The fighting in Korea contained all the horror of war, and it reflected all the brutal aspects of men and women fighting other men and women. It contained all the fear and danger so common for civilians caught between nations at war. Nothing that happened there is lessened by the euphemisms many have used to describe the action—rather than admit it was a war. However, the memory of what was done there, why it was done, and who did it to whom is easily lost in the failure to acknowledge the essence of what happened.

Sometimes war is the result of little more than the desire of an individual or a class to own or occupy something belonging to another. Sometimes it is the outcome of the desire to create an empire. While few would want to suggest that war is inevitable, it is difficult to imagine a situation in which justice is so apparent that war will not appear as necessary to someone.

The combat in Korea lasted thirty-seven months. The need to maintain a military alert and to defend the 38th Parallel continues today. The danger of hostile nations facing one another has lasted many years. Numerous nations fought under the aegis of the United Nations in this isolated and limited war, as did thousands of Chinese and millions of Koreans of varied political persuasion. The war in Korea took 54,200 American lives. More than a hundred thousand Americans were wounded in this war. Thousands were taken prisoner. Many persons identified as prisoners (POW) or missing in action (MIA) have never been identified or recovered. Both the Democratic People's Republic of Korea and the Republic of Korea suffered devastating economic breakdowns. Millions of refugees were uprooted from their homes, sometimes even their nations. The land was pocked by continual bombing and artillery. The nations suffered the loss of hydroelectric systems, the collapse of the infrastructure, and the failure of transportation and communication systems.

ACKNOWLEDGING THE KOREAN WAR

This book is an effort to acknowledge the Korean War. The hope is that by discussing some of the varied characteristics of the Korean War, rather than providing yet another narrative of the combat that ranged up and down the peninsula, the war can be better appreciated by persons who have not previously understood it. This is not an attempt to provide a final history, nor does the author maintain any pretense of providing answers to the many questions raised. Many highly qualified persons continue to produce more definitive narrative histories. Others work to address many of the questions that remain. The purpose of this work is to offer some thoughts about the peculiar nature of the Korean War and about the circumstances surrounding it. I have borrowed the philosopher's tool, and the result is an effort not so much to answer questions as to question some of the many answers we have learned to live with.

Many see the Korean War as a mystery. Some parts of it seem almost immune to study and understanding. Statistics tell us some things, and chronological narratives can provide us a story upon which to hang data and factual information. But the problem is simply that we still do not know very much about the war. It was so complex, both in terms of its causes, and of the progress of the fighting, that the usual methods of reporting do not always tell a clear story. It was (and is) a significant part of American history, and within it are located keys to understanding America's highly transitional role in the increasingly complex world events of the time. The hope is to develop an appreciation for what was accomplished during the Korean War, by taking a somewhat critical look at some of the more "acceptable," but not necessarily true, memories of the war.

The cease-fire brought the worst of the fighting to a close. But conflict continued, and continues today. It is still highly possible that large-scale hostilities will break out again. For nearly five decades, well-equipped armies have kept watch along that narrow strip of Korea known as "the demilitarized zone" (DMZ), a stretch of land 2.5 miles wide and 155 miles long across the peninsula. No closer to unification today than they were at the beginning of the war, the Korean people have gained little, other than a bitterness more intense than the bitterness that already existed. In anticipation of further conflict, thousands of men and women in the military have remained on the alert. During these years many people, some of them Americans, have died.

The big guns fell silent at 2200 hours on July 27,1953. United Nations military forces, spread across the width of Korea, breathed a little easier. The movement of troops fighting to occupy more territory came to a stop. The silent killing of patrols deep in the barren hills slowed and came to a close. At sea, the massive guns of the combined navies of the United Nations bombarded their targets inland, firing in a steady rhythm, until one minute before the appointed time. Then they stopped. Ships on blockade duty in Wonsan Harbor, and along the length of both coasts, hit targets and maneuvered to avoid return fire until the deadline arrived.

On the winding Kansas Line and Wyoming Line, which had seen so much action along the front, United Nations artillery units fired 105mm and 155mm shells into enemy target positions right up to the end. Scores of Navy and Marine planes rose from the carriers to carry out last-minute raids of interdiction and destruction. Fifth Air Force fighters and heavy bombers were sent aloft from the fields in Korea, Japan, and Okinawa on missions of destruction deep into the Communist territory. The planes returned just short of the cease-fire.

Because the Communist Chinese communication system was slow, the armistice provided a twelve-hour period for the word to spread to the widely scattered troops. During this period there was little, if any, attempt to curtail the war. The Communists appeared no less eager to end the killing than the United Nations. Communist mortar shells rained down on huddled troops with the same accuracy the Chinese had shown from the beginning. North Korean troops raided between the still-disputed hills, and landings were launched against offshore islands. Artillery shells burst in and between the American and United Nations commands right up to the final moment.

When the firing finally stopped, there was no great joy experienced in the field, as there had been at the armistice on November 11, 1918. There was no spontaneous outpouring of relief, or any great happiness expressed by the home front, as had been expressed upon the news of the end of World War II. The cease-fire in Korea brought little celebration. Few in Korea really thought it was over. Few believed that the job had been done. A good many felt that it would continue. For most, this was not a crusade against evil, not even against Communism; it was simply another job to be done. Having done the best they knew, veteran's felt little sense of accomplishment. No land had been occupied, no grand goals had been reached, no clear victory had established a winner, no surrender received to mark the end of the war. The fighting men and women were relieved to see the fighting stop. That was about all.

There had been many false hopes during the war. There had been many changes of policy as well as decisions made and then reversed. There had been several promises of getting home by Christmas. All involved had received a great deal of false information about who was involved and what they were fighting for. When the firing actually stopped and the troops were free to stand upright and move around, they were certainly grateful for the relief. But they were not overjoyed. David Halberstam suggested that while Americans tolerated the Korean War when it was being fought, they managed to forget it just as soon as it was over.

On the home front, very little notice was taken. The service of the veterans was never well acknowledged by the nation that had sent them. The war itself had been a violation, not only of the hard-won peace of World War II but of the world order and American domination that such a powerful victory seemed to have promised. The Korean War challenged the memory, and the memory was still paramount. The American solution was to let the reality of the Korean War waver and then disappear.

LIMITED WAR

In hindsight, it is easy to acknowledge that the Korean War was a major factor in establishing the modern concept of limited war. The Korean War represented one side of the search for an acceptable philosophy of war. The nations involved did not achieve their stated goals. Of them all, perhaps the Chinese came the closest. However, all the nations managed to avoid complete defeat, any major alteration of their national boundaries, or complete surrender. Few would say that the war in Korea started with limitations in mind. In fact, there is still considerable discussion about why the war started at all. But it became clear in the early days of 1951 that the continuation of the war, as well as the possibility of achieving any real victory, had become seriously entwined with changing ideals of political security and self-determination.

The medieval philosopher Niccolo Machiavelli, one of the more famous of the early advocates of war as a political tool, recommended limited war as a means of maintaining and expanding the influence of the state. While his view of war, and of everything else, was tempered by pragmatism, he did make an important point that is worth our consideration. There is never a very wide area of separation, he suggested, between war and politics, for in the ultimate sense, the goals and expectations are about the same.

Despite the practical implications of a limited war, as introduced in our century, such a belief makes a mockery of the long-assumed view of war as the fulfillment of God's will or the result of any other external or ahistorical force. The history of war shows the numerous occasions during which war has been legitimized by an affirmation that the ultimate goals were determined by God or had some divine inevitability. If the goals are seen as a necessary response to the call of God and the victorious achievement of those goals as fulfilling His will, then success in battle is divine. That is, victory elicits God's pleasure. Such a belief makes limited peace appear a violation of God's will, thus likely to invoke divine displeasure.

For those trying to explain the human involvement in war, the same kind of determinism is found in the idea that war is a disease. If one holds that war is a disease that no nation can avoid catching, limited war is a false cure. That a nation might decide to wage less than total war and, in fact, managed to limit the war, it suggests that war is not a disease but rather a choice that can be avoided. If men and women catch the war disease, what is the source of the antidote? At what point, as in the case of a god-ordered war or a disease-infected war, does the ultimate source of conflict change? Why?

Generally, those who see war as a disease are not happy with restraints. Their goal, like that of many peace organizations, is the eradication rather than limitation of war. It is when nations leave behind God and disease, and all the other extreme efforts to justify war, that they can allow the political implications to emerge. Limited war enforces the unromantic assumption that war is nothing more than a political instrument for the regulating of national and international systems.

For Machiavelli those who would provide a justification for war, and those who support limited war as a means of control, the legitimacy of any war stems from the value it renders to those who fight it. That is, while many persons may become engaged in war because of their primary convictions, war eventually takes on goals that are essentially pragmatic. In this understanding, men and women see war as legitimate because of the immediate value it produces. For many who study war, it has become easier to deal with the pragmatic, and harder to see war as the result of external forces, mystical movements, or divine values.

Among all the attitudes toward war, it is the pragmatic one that offers us the best hope of avoiding nuclear disaster. For with serious consideration, power brokers know that no conflict that destroys the aggressor or prevents political or economic gain can be considered legitimate. It is, at the very least, hard to see how such a war could be of any value to those involved. A nation usually enters a war in anticipation of great gain or, at the worst, the prevention of great loss. But the potential value that can be gained from a war lessens as the intensity of weapons increase. New and powerful weapons, like gas in World

War I, often give the aggressor an edge. But the edge is of value only if it results in fairly immediate victory.

What usually happens, however, is that the advanced weapon is quickly countered. The enemy matches and often exceeds its power. The new destructiveness curtails not only the value of the initial weapon but alters the essential values that can be gained from continuing the war.

EARLY LESSONS

During the Korean War, the fact that the Soviet Union had tested an atomic bomb altered the conditions under which the United States could consider the use of its own bombs. If the United States had used nuclear weapons in Korea, the war might have ended more quickly and even to our advantage. However, the anticipated political response to the use of such weapons made that far more costly. By the time we decided to get out, in fact, the cost had become greater than the values that had first taken the United States into the Korean War.

Looking back on the Korean War, it is fairly easy to say that the war was fought within the "doctrine of proportionality." The phrase in this case means that the weapons, tactics, and conduct of the war conformed to the value of the objectives being sought. The truth is that the ultimate goals were not so important that the United States was willing to invest in ever-increasing numbers of, as well as more violent, weapons. This fact, even if not acknowledged by those in power at the time, can be observed by recognizing the limited resources that the United States—and for that matter all of the members of the United Nations—were willing to commit to fighting it with any determination.

During the early period of the Korean War, two rather significant ideas began to dominate American policy makers. The truth of these ideas was illustrated by the war itself. The first realization was that even in the age of nuclear weapons it was possible to contain war. War could, when it was to the advantage of the nations involved, be restricted to a given area, limited to a particular time, and focused on ideological expectations and psychological intentions rather than on physical occupancy.

The second lesson was that the existence of nuclear weapons did not, in itself, provide America with the defense and security that it had believed was possible. What war in Korea was teaching America was that war was not ultimate. War did not need to be a total investment , the greatest or harshest commitment. That, of course, meant the reevaluating of conventional weapons. Also, such a view would quickly provide the justification for continuous military preparedness. It had become apparent that any nation that would maintain world power and independence must be prepared for both massive retaliation and limited prosecution.

The immediate lesson then was that the heavy bombers circling the world, ready to drop atomic weapons on anyone who would oppose or threaten the United States, were not sufficient to keep the peace. T. R. Fehrenbach, in his highly respected *This Kind of War* [Fehrenbach 1963:3], states it well: "Americans in 1950 rediscovered something that since Hiroshima they had forgotten; you may fly over a land forever; you may bomb it, atomize it, pulverize it, and wipe it clean of life–but if you desire to defend it, protect it, and keep it for civilization, you must do this on the ground the way the Roman legions did, by putting your young men in the mud."

War was still going to be necessary in some cases to settle minor disputes, or to address problems too small to risk total involvement. What seemed to come as a surprise to many politicians–and not a few military men–was that while it might still be necessary to fight some wars, they did not have to be won. That is, wars did not have to be won in the same manner that the military had customarily identified as victory. If winning was all that was important, then the massive weapons we had available might be brought into use. But if the purpose of the fight, as it became in Korea, was to show a presence, stem a tide, express a commitment, or to emphasize a demand, then massive force might not be needed. Thus, in the emergence of a war of limited goals and expectations America needed other means of fighting.

THREE PHASES OF WAR

The Korean War, which began with the invasion of the Republic of South Korea in June of 1950, can be more easily understood if we consider it as two, perhaps even three, wars. The first phase was between the United Nations and the Democratic People's Republic of North Korea. This period can be considered a victory for the United Nations. Surely there is no other word for the successful landing at Inchon in September 1950, the recapture of the South Korean capital of Seoul, and the approach, by Eighth Army on the west and X Corps on the east, to the Yalu. By the middle of November, the forces of the United Nations had scattered the troops of North Korea's army and occupied most of its territory. The goals of the United Nations, to drive the invader from South Korea, had been accomplished.

The second phase, which General of the Army Douglas MacArthur called "an entirely new war," began with the Chinese entry into the conflict. This phase must be considered much less successful. In the light of the goals established for the second stage of the war–to expel the Communist Chinese and to occupy and control the territory of North Korea–the war was a failure.

But somewhere during the second year of fighting, around November 1951, the nature of the goals changed again. This change may be sufficient to define a third phase of the war. The third phase was marked by the decision to take a defensive posture in Korea. After the defeat at the Chosin reservoir and the slow United Nations return to the 38th Parallel military victory seemed to be too great a goal. The war became one of attrition, not unlike World War I. The third phase was one of waiting, patrolling, skirmishing, destroying supplies, and attacking to kill rather than to occupy, and negotiating.

If the legitimate purpose of war is to create a more perfect peace, as some have suggested, then phase three of the Korean War was its most important. Certainly the long-term goals, as well as the short-term reactions, seemed to be more directed at an easing of the Cold War than at victory in Korea.

The decision made by President Harry S. Truman and his advisors to enter the war in defense of South Korea was one of major significance. Some historians believe it may have been predetermined by earlier events leading up to the invasion. On the surface, however, the decision looks like a rather abrupt shift in the administration's policy concerning Korea. The reaction gave Korea more importance than it had previously held for Americans. Later, when Truman authorized General MacArthur to move across the 38th, and seek the occupation of North Korea, that decision did not appear so much out of character. In the final analysis, however, this latter decision introduced a period of military defeat, public concern, and political difficulty.

There is much about the fighting during the Korean War that, in an overview, appears paradoxical. The tremendous technological advances made during World War II paid off between 1945 and 1955. Weapon development moved quickly and weapons became more and more complex. Nevertheless, the Korean War was primarily fought with weapons left over from World War II. To a significant degree it was also fought with the strategies ,and often with the commanders, of that war. It was war fought in the beginning by untrained and unprepared occupation troops, then by "retreads" (recalled World War II veterans), then by draftees caught up in one of the loosest conscription nets in modern history. Of course, it was a war in which military methodology and expectancy were severely limited. Finally, we can say that the Korean War verified Clausewitz's understanding that a limited war can be true to its defined goals only as long as it remains subject to political (civilian) control.

HISTORY AND HISTORIES

The first phase of the war, the more successful phase, has received most attention from historians. The morbid truth of American military history–that we usually enter a war unprepared and thus suffer some initial defeats that tests our character–is fairly well defined and recorded. Some excellent work has been done on the invasion unleashed by the Democratic People's Republic of Korea. The early defeat of the Republic of Korea and the less than successful initial involvement of American troops has been extensively related. There have also been some rather detailed studies of the defense of the Pusan perimeter, the successful invasion at Inchon, and the effective Chinese trap into which American troops of X Corps fell at the Chosin Reservoir. The Marine "retreat in the opposite direction" and the evacuation at Hungnam have also been fairly well documented, even beautifully described. Of this early period, the planning and execution of the Inchon landing has received some of the best treatment.

Most other things about the war have, however, for some undefined reason, been strangely ignored or poorly covered. The ground-support role of the U.S. Air Force, the contributions of U.S. Navy bombardment and allied carrier forces, and the role of the Marine forces have all been considered to some extent. What appears to be missing from the narrative history of the Korean War is that phase known as the "hill war." It was in this final phase, which lasted longer and cost more in terms of lives and equipment, that the war broke down to its most basic elements. This was a period in which the "limited" character of the war took on its ugly form. So sensitive did the political situation become that the simplest of land operations required permission from the highest headquarters. During this period the individual hills, strongly contested, became bargaining chips in the armistice game.

Understandably, the majority of early interpretations of the war have been orthodox. The orthodox view records the Korean War as a necessary one, and provides massive support for the actions of the United States and the Republic of South Korea. These histories defend the positions and behavior of the United Nations, and the political and military stands they took. There were some early exceptions, which found fault in the American position, but the orthodox view was paramount.

In the 1960s and 1970s, probably spurred on by the Vietnam War but following a national trend, revisionist historians began to appear. The revisionist's role is to look with fresh eyes and offer new facts to offset historical views they feel are wrongly, or too hasty, held. The methodology is to dig deeply into aspects that may have been glossed over by earlier authors. Two or three characteristics identify the revisionist mode. One is skepticism concerning cause and effect. A second is a softening of the line between enemy and friend, and a willingness to learn from, and on occasion even to celebrate, the wisdom or success of the enemy. A third is an antiheroic view that tends to blame one's own nation for a war.

The 1960s and 1970s revisionism on Korea certainly has been altered and adjusted by the recent opening of Soviet archives, as well as limited access to materials in Communist China and North Korea. As more records have become available, such as through the translations and analysis provided by Kathryn Wethersby of the Woodrow Wilson International Center, several things have become more clear.

Among these is that Communist China most probably did not enter the war in the late 1950s as an act of aggression. Rather, it was responding to American pressure and its own desire for national recognition. The U.S. support of the Nationalist Chinese government during the latter part of the Chinese civil war, the support of the island stronghold of Formosa, and the decision to send American troops across the 38th Parallel to the very borders of Communist China all forced the issue.

Korea has long been considered America's "forgotten war." Many historians at least would acknowledge that it has not received the attention such an important conflict deserves, but it can no longer be considered forgotten. The word "ignored" seems to describe better how America has addressed the war. As this Asian war begins to take its place in history, there are many attributes of the war that remain to be addressed. To a large extent the American people ignored it during the fighting, and they have generally not remembered it since then. Ignored certainly, forgotten probably–even these images are changing. More and more people are beginning to recognize the important role the Korean War played in the Cold War.

ADDRESSING THE ISSUE

This work begins with a look at the long silence that has surrounded the Korean War. This silence is a matter not just of lack of memory but in some respects appalling ignorance. Philosophically, an important case can be made for the impact of naming in history. The lack of a meaningful name–was it a war, a conflict, a police action?–is partially responsible for the lack of historical analysis.

Since most people still tend to believe that wars are caused by specific events, we will look at the events behind the opening invasion. The question of responsibility for the Korean War is a far more complex question. This inquiry will take a look at some the details of this issue of responsibility.

The Korean War, like all wars, created a great deal of controversy. Among the disputes are the questions of legality; the United Nations decision to moved its troops north of the 38th Parallel; the use, or lack of use, of the atomic bomb; and MacArthur's dismissal. One of the questions is why only Inchon, and to some degree Chosin, are remembered, when the war produced several major battles and some highly interesting operations.

General Douglas A. MacArthur is certainly the best remembered military leader of the Korean War. But General MacArthur was not necessarily the leader people imagined he was: He was neither God nor devil, and he was not the most involved. The same selectivity we use in remembering leaders we also apply to our memory of those who actually fought the war. Reading what is available, it is tempting to think the Korean War was fought primarily by the First Marine Division. Others tend to believe it was conducted by fighter pilots stationed in Japan. In reality, the war was fought primarily by the U. S. Army, supported by more than twenty UN member nations, who supplied troops, ships, supplies, medical units, air squadrons, and transports. While the marines must be acknowledged for their contribution and courage, the army, navy– including the submarine service–and the newly organized U.S. Air Force each played a role. Forgotten as well have been the roles of the partisans, guerrilla groups, and special forces.

This brief inquiry concludes with a look at the question of "necessity." Applied to the study of war, necessity usually addresses the possibility that the war could have been avoided in the first place. Some wars, like the American Revolution, appear to have been matters of necessity. The force of history, the dynamics, passions and ideologies of that period, as well as the revolutionary spirit that was sweeping the world all seemed to produce the war of independence. Historians often feel this way about the unfolding drama of World War I, which, in looking back, appears to have been incapable of being prevented. In many ways this is true of World War II, the last of the "'big wars" that is considered to have been necessary.

Certainly some argument can be made that the emergence of the Cold War meant that the two major powers, the United States and the Soviet Union, would clash at some point. Why the conflict came to a boil in Korea, and why it happened when it did, are some of the significant questions that still need analysis.

The other side of the argument is that of contingency. Contingency, in this case, suggests that a war was not made necessary by predetermining forces. That is, at some moment the war in Korea could have been prevented. Some even go so far as to argue that it was not determined by events but staged by men for particular purposes. Both of these views help us to understand why so many have misidentified General of the Army Omar Bradley's famous remark, "The wrong war, at the wrong time, with the wrong enemy." In fact General Bradley was talking about war with Communist China, but the quote fits the Korean situation. Was the war in Korea (1950-53) necessary? Was the war with the right (correct) enemy? Was it even important?

At the end of this book is a listing of the works used in the preparation of and referred to in the work. The list is mainly of secondary sources. There are many fine works not mentioned; this listing is not meant as a judgment on the value of the works. It is simply a matter of space. The books that are listed are generally still available to the average reader.

I have purposely kept the documentation and references to a minimum, and within the text, in an effort to make the work easier to read. Textual references (by source and page, in square brackets) are identified and there are recommendations for further reading. My hope is to produce a series of essays rather than a research effort. There is no intent to slight any author whose works I have consulted or ideas I have described. I trust all concerned will accept that I acknowledge the great debt I owe others and that my reference to them result from my respect for them and their work.

Many scholars are now entering the field of the Korean War. A number of fine historians have written fairly complete histories of this important conflict. The recent availability of new sources means that the best works are still to come. The limited number of good narrative histories is not a reflection on the work of military historians, but rather of the lack of available monographs. The field is young, despite the years that have passed. Historians who wish to write narrative histories need an abundance of highly specialized and deeply researched articles for almost every area. These specialized inquiries, and the careful analyses they represent, are the bread and butter of future narrative histories.

In general, there does appear to be a real increase in the acknowledgment, and understanding, of the Korean War. Within the last few years there have been several M.A. theses and PhD dissertations the field. Before that, there were hardly any. Also the professional journals are getting either more manuscripts concerning the war or their editors are aware either of a new interest in the Korean War, for the number of articles on various aspects of the war seems to be increasing. The *Journal of Military History* has done an excellent job of publishing materials on the Korean War. Publishing houses like Garland, Texas A& M Press, Anvil, and to a larger measure Greenwood Press have increased the number of titles available.

The second positive note is found in the expansion of archival materials now becoming available as a result of the opening of the Soviet archives. While not as open as they once were, a good deal of new materials has surfaced from the Soviets. Not only have some of the old Communist nations made their records available, but the British, and American governments have released a lot of information. Communist materials, which have always been difficult to use because of the language problem, are being translated and analyzed.

A brief comment is in order about the conflict that sometimes exists between the military historian, the "academic historian," and the amateur. Many uniformed historians have special access to materials, as well as attitudes and abilities that make them excellent historians. Academic historians have the learned skills and expertise to do fine history. The third group, the amateurs, quite often has the advantages of focus and passion. These men and women research and write out of love for the story; what they lack in expertise and experience they make up in dedication. All have places in the business of understanding the Korean War. The conflict between them is often more one of ego than intellect. Fortunately, cooperation seems to be growing. Much of the material needed to understand this war remains in the minds, hearts, and records of individual soldiers. Its discovery will require historians, amateur and professional, to join their efforts.

Chapter 2

The Long Silence

Not until America began to realize the magnitude of the mistake
it had made in Vietnam would it be able to put Korea in perspective.

Richard Severo

Historian Joseph Goulden once identified the Korean War as an unattractive subject. Since it ended, he acknowledged, it has become a period in American history that most Americans have been very happy to see slip through the cracks of history. In many respects he appears to be right. But the silence associated with the war represents more than simply forgetting. It is also a sign of rejection.

The cease-fire documents that ended the fighting in Korea were signed on July 27, 1953. The more than forty-five years since that event have been characterized as a long and awkward period of silence about the war. Over the years, the lack of attention has been exaggerated by the common acceptance of the term "forgotten war" to describe an event that has suffered many misnomers. This term, usually credited to General Matthew Ridgway, has been used so often it has become a name as well as a description.

During World War II, the American people clearly understood the goals and expectations of the war they were fighting. In the simplest terms, the war was fought in Europe to defend democracy, and in the Pacific in the pursuit of revenge. Most Americans saw World War II as a good war. The war clearly was politically necessary and morally valid. The principles involved were basic, and the United States was not only justified but obligated to meet and defeat the enemies of mankind.

The conflict in Vietnam was seen by many Americans from the opposite view point. The goals in Vietnam were never clearly defined. American involvement was to be the cause of considerable disruption in the political core of the United States. This war was seen by many as an act of imperialism and, under the best of circumstances, as morally and politically corrupt.

The Korean War was chronologically located between World War II and

Vietnam, and it was balanced emotionally in the American mind between a war of principle and an act of imperialism. It was not supported, as was World War II, nor did it suffer the condemnation of Vietnam. It was an unpopular war that disturbed the nation politically, though not enough to be so remembered. Though hardly recognized at the time, the Korean War was the beginning of a transition from one kind of thinking about America's wars to a new, more critical, consideration.

Much of what is to be learned about, and from, the war is to be found in the manner in which the event is recorded in cultural history. For it is in literature, the theater, music, poetry, and film that the creative imagination of the nation records its comprehension of what has happened. This culture is the source of recall for those involved, as well as for the generations yet to come. Caught between the good and the bad, the Korean War–an ideological war with undefined goals–is considered by many the watershed of America's eventual decline.

There are many reasons why the Korean War has been labeled "forgotten." Some of the reasons are psychological, and some are emotional. Some reasons might be more easily identified as political or social. Whatever the reason, it is probably important to acknowledge that the term "forgotten" is often self-fulfilling. That is, such a view may well be the cause for some of the lack of memory. When it is used to discuss the Korean War, the term "forgotten" means more than simply a person "forgets" to do something. It is more than a bad memory. To a very large extent, the Korean War has been *ignored.* This sad fact has been no better expressed than by the comment of the art curator at the Army Center for Military History, who tells us there has been "no organized effort by either the Army or the private sector, to visually capture the Korean War, so the Army's collection has relatively few images of that war"[as quoted in Kerin 1994:49].

The word *ignored* implies some effort to reject, or put aside, strong memories of the war. This is not the result of a "conspiracy." Conspiracy is far too strong a word, and it implies some sort of calculated misdeed, for which little evidence exists. The rejection is, rather, the result of a lack of serious concern by politicians, educators, historians, military people, and quite often by bureaucrats "with an attitude." The nation selects its memories, through affirmation and commemoration. In ignoring these tools, nations forget.

James Kerin has written, "Although poles apart in the nature of their remembered images, the two world wars and Vietnam at least occupy positions of relative consensus within the American cultural memory. For the Korean War that is not so"[Kerin 1994:42]. The Korean War stands outside, and it is best described by void, or absence. Until recently there were no recognized monuments. The war lacks any significant poetry, it has produced only a few novels, and it spawned few if any worthwhile films. But more than that, there is no myth, no story. It is quite often left out of the recitation of America's past affirmations.

It is not just in America that the Korean War has suffered silence, but also in Great Britain, Canada, France, Australia, New Zealand–and, we are discovering, in China. Bin Yu, a professor of political science whose credentials include service in the People's Liberation Army, has raised an interesting point. In "What China Learned from Its 'Forgotten War' in Korea" [Bin 1998:4-16] , he reports that there is a new thirst for materials about the Korean War. It is more than historical curiosity or veteran's nostalgia in China, but a new respect for what should have been learned there.

Once the cease-fire was established, the People's Liberation Army began to suffer some domestic upheavals that led in 1959 to a purge of its the leadership by Mao Tse-tung. In the 1960s there occurred a shift toward what was called "spiritual refinement." This internal conflict was followed by the long Sino-Soviet split. For more than forty years, the pressure of other, more pressing events meant that the Korean War was primarily ignored–even forgotten–in China.

The fact that the national conflict is once again being considered, Bin Yu suggests, has "something to do with the shift in the People's Liberation Army's (PLA) strategic thinking since the mid-1980s, when the PLA turned its attention from preparing to fight total war to dealing with ones that were limited and localized in scope" [Bin 1998:4-16]. The Chinese are taking a whole new look at the Korean War, because it has become evident that serious lessons can be learned from the it.

At the same time, the official Chinese position on the start of the war has been rather significantly redefined. There is a growing tendency to blame the North Korean government. The Chinese are not letting the United States off the hook, but it no longer blames either America or South Korea for initiating the war. Perhaps more important, the Chinese since 1990 have made it clear that while they continued to favor the unification of Korea, they would support such a move only if made peacefully and reasonably.

COMMEMORATION

It was nearly half a century after the Korean War broke out in July 1996, that the Korean War Veterans Memorial was dedicated in Washington, D.C. Even then, most veterans were not interested in fighting the war once again, nor were many concerned with arguing its merits. As citizens, they simply wanted to make a connection between the present and the past they understood and to maintain that connection in a personal and efficient way. The war was remembered, when remembered, as a mixture of anguish and apathy. For many veterans the memorial was too little; for some it was too late. For others, the memorial represented a significant beginning to the long-overdue task of locating the Korean War in American history.

In any commemorative effort, there often emerges a gap, sometimes even a tension, between those who were involved and those now in positions of community responsibility. The distance exists between those who suffered the consequences of the events being remembered, and individuals who see the memorial as a means of defending the national identity and experience. Public memory is created out of this tension between the needs of the nation (as seen by those who assume responsibility for the nation) and the anguish of those living the memory and seeking adequate and sufficient recognition. If the personal view wins, the event becomes localized and reduced to the memories of immediate events; the commemoration misses their place, however heroic, in the life of the nation.

If the official view wins, it defends the political base against ideas (memories) seen as threats against the nation's attainments and goals. For instance, we can acknowledge now the purpose of the American Bicentennial Commission: it was the job of the commission to convince the American people that the social, political, and economic problems they now faced, 200 years later, could be solved by existing organizations and programs. One of the great successes of the American Civil War Commemoration Committee was its rather unique ability to identify with both the particular vernacular passions of the local citizen and the patriotic language of larger national loyalties.

National trauma often reaffirms emerging national identity, provides an opportunity to acknowledge the standards that the nation holds sacred to its existence. Traditionally, national memory begins with commemorative events–the ticker-tape parade or bands waiting at the dock and continues with the building of memorials and the declaration of holidays. These memorial acts consolidate the events of the past and give them concrete, as well as shadow, memories–memories that will serve as cornerstones for the building of future configurations. But in order for these often traumatic events to take their proper places in the social and cultural life of the nation, they must be remembered; memory makers might well be willing to forget events which they somehow believe shame the people and the nation.

In trying to deal with the past, human beings are often caught between two realities. On the one hand is the narrative by which each of us explains who we are to others and to ourselves. On the other hand is the sense of reality that lives deep within us and, on occasion, challenges the stories we tell ourselves. During that confrontation, the need for reality demands comparison between the narrative and the truth. Such bifurcation is one reason why psychotherapy has become almost as common as haircuts; it is also why nations often find it difficult to account for their behavior, even as they live out the effects of that behavior. When nations, like individuals, try to rewrite the past in such a way as to ignore its impact, they are likely to become sick, and their affirmations to become obsessions.

People and nations require historical understanding if they are to explain the varied perspectives from which they view events, and to construct reasoned alternatives in response [Archibald 1994:11]. For the discipline of history to take its proper role in the analysis of past events, those events must be readdressed and reevaluated in each new generation: there is a great deal of truth in the idea that the only duty we owe to history is to rewrite it. But the point of this effort is to learn from what we have experienced, not to write out, or avoid, those stories in which we may appear in a poor light. When nations try to write their history so as to exclude the generally unacceptable, they are predestined to repeat their largest mistakes.

EDUCATION

In America, the study of military history has declined. The decline appears to have begun at the point at which the narrative ceased to be a source of national pride. Its beginning was, or was at least coincidental with, the Korean War. Sensing that things in America had become less than perfect, the nation acted like any "normal neurotic." The people searched for some form of self-analysis, in order to see what might be wrong. Experience, however, has made it fairly evident that seeking to understand significant issues of history while at the same time avoiding them, will not help a great deal. The result of our self-analysis has been that America has moved into an internalized, class-centered, and multiethnic view of history, sometimes called "environmental" history.

When military history is taught in American schools these days, it is caught in an interesting juxtaposition between those who maintain wars are *ahistorical* and those for whom they are *post-historical*. The first group considers the Korean War as an imposed event; they feel the Korean War arose out of context, as if dropped by some outside force into the process of time. It was not the result of a long series of previous events. Nor do they see the Korean War as a cause of subsequent events. They would present the Korean War as a single event rather than a link in the chain of time. In the educational situation, they link the event only with the other events of the time, rather than trying to understand what happened before and after. This attitude is supported–and in some way is strengthened–by the way the teachers, not having themselves been taught about this war, tend to look it up as an isolated item in the index of a source book.

On the other hand, some within the educational system have adopted the *post-historical* view. This attitude has been strengthened by the conflict in Vietnam. Its effect is that the results of Vietnam have written back into the causes and characters of previous events. This allows people to use the Vietnam experience as a philosophical model, a "first principle," of the American society. Such a view is reflected in the whole range of psychological and sociological, rather than the military, understandings of the Vietnam War that have been transposed into responses to the Korean War. Some educators "explain" Korea by recounting the ills that plagued the nation during Vietnam. The two extremes of the view are reflected in the Rambo movies, reflecting an urge to "do it right this time," and the national acceptance of "post-traumatic stress syndrome," which plays so quickly into our national guilt.

EDUCATION AS SOURCE

In the last half-century or so, events of the past have often been dismissed as more representative of "memory" than of "meaning" [Stearn 1993:135]. Thus, we are often found searching for meaning not in what has happened but in the coincidences of separate environments, special emphases, and cultural explanations. We have recently given in to the tendency to pull our history apart in an effort to establish a pattern among the pieces: the American educational system has bought into the idea that the character of the stew is to be found in the essence of the individual vegetables. Out of a sense of national guilt—guilt for having been successful and reasonably happy—we have elected to "embrace the villain within" and moved toward a separate-but-equal concept of history. This environmentalization of history has occurred before, but never in such breadth or for so long. Nor have the historical disciplines been so dominated by inquiries in such limited and unrelated fields.

The failure of the American education system adequately to consider the Korean War may be partially explained, though not justified, by the wide variety of difficulties and issues involved. Not the least of the difficulties is the fact that neither history nor the subject of history itself is taken very seriously in our school systems. These days we are often told that history is not relevant. Jacques Barzun used to tell the story of a history course advertised as "specially designed for those who do not feel equal to the demands of regular history." Unfortunately, this describes a good deal of what passes for history these days. To a large extent it has been rewritten, reinterpreted, or selectively remembered for the sake of political correctness and to appease a national lack of self-confidence.

Though teachers must accept some of the blame, they are not totally at fault. Well-meaning school boards have put them in a particularly difficult position. The faculty is often expected to maintain a cautious peace between historical methods and a wide variety of cultural, ethnic, and social "realities." There are political ramifications even in the selection of what is to be taught. In our "weathervane society," with its stated need to respond to every social wind that blows, the assumption has developed that history can somehow be taught without a point of view. Thus, it is "safer" to give in to the American predilection to substitute social studies for history. It also reflects pressure to make a significant number of environmental and ethnic concessions before a topic is even considered.

The application of selective remembrance and the substitution of "data points" for integration means that the flow of history has been broken. It is so broken that we find it difficult to make the connection between cause and effect. Thomas Leckey has provided an excellent illustration in his comments on Kevin Costner's movie *Dances with Wolves:* taken as a narrative, the movie "gives us a beautiful, moving example of the latest trend in popular history, revision as therapy, or history as psychoanalysis" [Leckey 1991: 88]. In that film the hero, fresh to the frontier, has just fought in the American Civil War in order, among other things, to free the slaves. Now, apparently unaware of what he has done, our hero finds himself facing the consequences of his victory. He does not see the significant relationship between the freeing of the slaves and the rather sudden appearance in the West of unemployed southern farmers (white and black) seeking workable land. The result is increased tension between the Indians and the United States government. It is this demand for new land that will bring the powerful and tragic culmination of the struggle between the conflicting cultures that had begun centuries before.

History is the record of cultures under strain. When the interests of one body grate upon those of another, there will be some give, but the tensions will stretch like the earth along a fault line. When the pressure grows too great, some often minor irritation releases the strain, and a massive quake results. Such moments are often identified as wars. Like the earthquakes they resemble, they are not ahistorical. Rather, they are the results of the constant tension between vast, moving forces. When they move the results are not so much different as sudden. True, war often speeds up the process, but it does not necessarily alter the trend. Wars are eruptions. But wars are not violations of the historical process.

The Indians with whom Costner identified were native Americans only in the sense that they had been on the plains before the white man. But we know that the land to which they were attached had, in turn, been taken from other, more native, Americans. The Plains Indians of 1870 had stolen much of the land they claimed, in much the same manner as the U. S. Army was shown doing in the Costner's film. To study wars as if they were separate topics or isolated events outside of history, or simply to ignore them, is to violate not only the history of the events but the nature of history itself.

AN INADEQUATE STORY

By ignoring the Korean War, Americans have violated the heritage they have tried so hard to build. We have not taken advantage of the many, and serious, lessons to be learned from the war. We have, in ignoring this significant event, diminished much of the hope of better behavior in the future. The teaching of the Korean War might well be difficult. That is understandable. In fact, it would be a nightmare to those needing some politically correct presentation. Currently, Korean War history is being taught, if taught at all, using the current thesis that "accuracy is not only inconvenient but gets in the way of feelings. "Ain't it better," asks Wesley Purden, "to make a kid dumb and happy instead of smart and sad?" What so many educators fail to understand is that many students, having no adequate explanation for their heritage, remain both dumb and sad [Purden 1992:17].

The story often told these days in place of history does not seem to explain who or what we are. The story of America, minus the events in Korea, does not account for the behavior of the nation. It does not identify many of our fears and obsessions. What is lacking in our educational system is not simply the facts of this particular war (though the presentation of those facts would be an excellent beginning) but rather realization that themes, threads, processes, human nature, and the ever-present force of change drive people, and nations into action. When these beliefs are isolated from the events and attitudes that created them, they appear to have emerged in a historical vacuum. They seem to have been catastrophically dropped into our history, without rhyme or reason. Thus we generally fail to see them in context and fail to heed the sound dictum that historical judgments are best discovered, not dictated.

Because we often lack background information many of our current international involvements appear very complex and our relationships are often unfathomable. Many of our modern policies and expectations for success are poorly defined. Many of the decisions being made today seem grossly unwise. Understanding the Korean War is not going to solve all this; Today's world is far better understood from the overall perspective of the Cold War. But if we understood it better, we might be able to relate better to many of today's headlines.

The fighting itself was primarily conventional and often, as in most wars, more boring than dramatic. Our soldiers fought as UN troops but the multinational dimension was limited. The society in which they fought was unfriendly, and the casualties (as often from cold and disease as from bullets and bombs) were massive but unspectacular in number. Yet, any belief today that it was an ordinary war emerges from the misconception in the American education system that the Korean War was a minor incident, if notable at all.

One way to discern the current status of the Korean War in educational circles is to look at the textbooks available for the teaching of American history. Irwin Z. Braun and Robert McCullough recently surveyed secondary-school textbooks [Braun 1998:47-48]. While not without serious faults in methodology, the study reveals some important information. According to it, the average American history textbook devotes only forty-nine lines to the Korean War: that is about one page. The vast majority (82 percent) provide a map of some sort. All of the books checked contain some mention of the war, and all identify the Democratic People's Republic of Korea as the aggressor. A very small percentage (9 percent) mention the role of the Soviet Union. Two-thirds of the books (65 percent) fail to note the relationship between the Korean War and the Cold War. The same number fail to mention the costs of the war in terms of casualties or to mention the more than eight thousand prisoners of war who have not yet been located.

Half of the books checked do not identify the major battles of the war, the drastic defeat at Chosin, the holding action at Pusan, the victory at Inchon. President Truman's firing of General MacArthur makes it into nearly two-thirds (63 percent) of the textbooks, with some going into considerable detail. There is more reflection on the constitutional questions raised than on the military ones, yet not one of these books discusses the fact that President Truman took America into war in Korea without the approval of the Congress.

Of those checked, 90 percent associate the war with the United Nations. None of the works–and this seems incongruous–mention the fact that the U. S. military was integrated by this time.

Perhaps the most interesting statistic Braun and McCullough show is that fewer than three-quarters (73 percent) of the textbooks mention that the war came to a close as the result of a cease-fire, not a peace settlement. Even fewer of the books discuss the Demilitarized Zone (DMZ) or postwar problems with North Korea.

HISTORY AND LITERATURE

The problem extends beyond textbooks, however. The interested person seeking information about the Korean War, or the casual reader trying to understand the history of the nation, soon discovers there are few books to enlighten him or her. Certainly, the number of books available on the Korean War is small when compared to other military events. Some of the few that are available are excellent. Many, however, are reprints of books written forty years ago, a good portion of which quote from each other.

A quick survey of the bookstores in any metropolitan area will show that there is not much interest in–or at least not much material on–the Korean War. A brief and unofficial survey recently conducted at three of the major franchised bookstores in Kansas City, Missouri, discovered that one retailer had seven works on the Korean War, and one had five. The others, while they had sections marked for Korean War books, had filled the area with books on Vietnam. These numbers compare to the estimated one hundred works available on Vietnam, three long bookcase sections on World War II, and considerably more than that concerning the Civil War.

The number of Korean War poetry, short stories, novels, academic works, and even films is small indeed. There is little to compare with World War II novels like Norman Mailer's *The Naked and the Dead* (1948). While the fiction of World War II was less upbeat than the public image of the war, it retained a sense of value and a patriotic image. Korean War novels, and there are few to consider, tend to reflect despair.

What novels, films, plays, and poetry have been produced share the ambivalence with which so many saw the war. The question of validity is hardly ever considered in World War II literature; Vietnam literature, and there is a great deal of it, appears to assume fairly easily a "bad war" tone. The Korea material is more realistic, the language hard, the views cynical, but it rarely provides any clear understanding of the value and/or purpose of the war. The American reaction is rather well stated in an otherwise mediocre book, *The Secret*. The "Korean War," the author tells us, "was a blinding nightmare of muck, blood, strange and slant-eyed faces both in front trying to kill us and behind us begging from us, offering us women and wine for money" [Drought 1963:140]. It was the experience, not the war, that was recorded.

James Hickey, author of one of the few really good novels of the Korean

War, tells us that most Korean veterans are quiet, graying men, who are inclined to remember mostly–or at least tell someone about–the hills, the heat, and the cold. He will mention the "mortars maybe, but mainly the hills–the goddamned hills." Trying to explain why the Korean War has produced so little literature, Hickey suggests that veterans "didn't want to talk about it, or perhaps no one wanted to listen" [Kerin 1994:177]. The insightful author Paul Fussell finds that the Korean War "generated virtually no literature." Bruce Cumings suggests that for a good many the war is a hazy memory buried in history. Peter Jones believes that "the literature of the Korean War is slight in both volume and quality, a situation probably explained to a large degree by the absence of a national commitment to the war" [Kerin 1994:178-179]. Although the war managed to produced some significant debate between liberals and conservatives, the war was not a meaningful symbol for either.

Poetry has never been a characteristically American reaction, though there is considerable poetry of merit from both world wars and the fighting in Vietnam. Paul Fussell tells us that the First World War had a distinctly literary quality in Europe but not so in the United States, primarily because it was not really a participant. World War II was different, generating some significant poetry both from the field and at home. This is also true, to a lesser degree, of Vietnam. It is efforts to identify and collect some of the scattered materials that have uncovered some serious Korean War poetry.

Perhaps more telling is that little came out of the Korean War that reflected the popular culture: no songs like "My Buddy" from World War I, or "Praise the Lord and Pass the Ammunition" of World War II, nor, skipping a war, like the popular Arlo Guthrie song "Alice's Restaurant."

What other ages have memorialized in books the modern age often places in films. But the film industry did little to record the Korean War. The American film acknowledged its historical and narrative function as World War II pushed America into a position of global prominence. The movies, "by reflecting the times and playing to what they think are the desires of their audiences–tend to be a good portrayal of what is important to the film makers of the time. They inadvertently tell us a lot about what is important" [Biskind 1983:5]. As it turns out, the film memory of the Korean War–often little more than recycled scripts and footage from World War II–is reflective of the apathy and discontent of the 1950s, thus it is of little significance as a source for calling a new generation to remembrance.

The films that emerged during and from the Korean War used primarily the same format of as those of World War II. This was true even of Sam Fuller's *Steel Helmet*, one of the better films. The Korean War films were World War II films with a different foe. The Korean veteran had his own "pinup": Marilyn Monroe, nicknamed Miss Flame-Thrower. There was also the United Services Organization (USO). Bob Hope, with a dedication appreciated by most GIs, was a steady force in a weakening USO effort. In fact, he greatly embarrassed the First Marine Division when as a guest of the ROK army, he greeted it when it landed in October 1951. Yet this sort of home-front involvement never got off the ground. Hollywood briefly supported an entertainment fund to performances stateside for Korea-bound troops. It was the basis of the B-class movie called *Starlife* (1951). The project was only funded with five thousand dollars, and was quickly out of business.

Korean literature appears "relegated to a limb-like existence between two other wars that, for entirely different reasons and in entirely different ways, captured on a grand scale the interests of the society and the imagination of many of its writers" [Kerin 1994:271]. During the Korean War about 350 correspondents were accredited to the United Nations command. Eighteen combat journalists were killed. Voluntary censorship did not work nearly as well in Korea as it had during World War II. There was little or no illusion among the journalists about the success of the United Nations effort. But it must be remembered that the press was subsidized: they traveled free, at the cost of the government; they were given uniforms; they could transmit their stories free; and they were shepherded about by the public information officers and given almost daily briefings. Many of the stories reported were the same, appearing under different bylines in different cities.

The partnership between the military and the correspondents crumbled, however, as the war moved along. Tension increased. Some of the journalists had covered World War II and found the experience vastly different. Correspondent Reginald Thompson found that the primary feeling was one of ambivalence about the war.

In his play *The Rack*, Rod Serling wrote, "At best Korea seemed to be an inconclusive muddled and bloody affair that we were unable to win and couldn't afford to lose." The memory of the war appears about as confused. While it is difficult to understand why some things are remembered and others are not, one thing has emerged from the long silence: the failure of memory makes analysis difficult. The primary "purpose of historical analysis," as Peter Stearn points out, lies in "examining relationships between one period and the next and assessing the nature and magnitude of change." This cannot happen, he warns us—and he has been proven right—if those concerned show little experience in "applying the analysis to contemporary situations" [Stern 1993:A32].

Because of the lack of analysis, an abundance of intellectual as well as moral questions about the war remain—questions that are not only unanswered but unaddressed. Today, as this war continues, with nations still facing each other along an armed front, we need to acknowledge that all that was achieved was a cease-fire between armies, not a peace treaty. It is time to consider the impact of this war on American and world history. Without identification, it is very difficult to compare events of the Korean War with either past or present.

Historian Samuel Eliot Morrison claimed in the 1960s that the Korean War had been a victory for the United States and the United Nations. The American intervention had stopped a major Communist lunge southward and most likely had been the reason that Japan had avoided the engulfing tide of communism. The war had made it clear to the Communists that the United Nations was more than a paper tiger, and that it could, and if necessary would, fight. He declared that in hindsight the Korean War, despite the cost in lives and funds, had been significant. The statement, however, lacks the benefit of analysis of the last thirty years. He blamed the Republicans in the U.S. Senate for assuming the effort was a failure. This may well be too hard on the Republicans, though there is little doubt they led the effort to disengage the American people from the Korean War and its outcomes.

The memories of World War II, like Vietnam, are still very much present in the American consciousness. In contrast there is a tendency to forget the Korean War. It is probably true that it is easier to remember the victories and the brave, if embarrassing, defeats. But a war that produced little more than a stalemate may not be worth remembering. When the Korean War ended, the boundaries were drawn about where they had been when it started. The war was not looked upon as a "real war" but only as a "police action" conducted by many nations under the direction of United Nations. Despite the fierce battles of the war and the more than 150,000 American casualties, the Korean War does not seem to have produced the pain and suffering that many people feel make an event worth remembering. It has never been truly celebrated.

Writing thirty years later but still trying to make the best case, popular historian John Toland wrote, "The forgotten war may eventually turn out to have been the decisive conflict that started the collapse of communism. In any case, those who fought did not fight and die in vain" [Toland 1991:3]. There are many who believe this, but the memory so far has not supported it.

Chapter 3

Naming The War

It will be seen that the control of the past depends
above all on the training of the memory.

George Orwell

Some of the mystery surrounding the Korean War is due to the fact that it has
never been properly identified. The confusion about what it should be called
reflects the considerable differences of opinion about what it was. The
situation is confusing, and without clear identification the war–and in every
sense it was a war–cannot be placed in the proper classification. We have
learned it is by classification that men and women use for the purpose of
definition and memory. When addressing something new, people narrow it
down, locate it within the context of something they already understand, and
identify it in relationship to other items in that same category.

Thus without some classification there is little hope of clear memory, nor
is there any possibility of meaningful analysis. A good portion of the vague
and massive misunderstanding about Americans' involvement in Korea
results from the fact that we have never been able to determine, or agree, how
to "think about" the Korean experience.

The German philosopher Friedrich W. Nietzsche (1844 -1900) was the
first modern intellectual to acknowledge the close tie between naming
something and remembering it. For the purpose of identification and
memory, Nietzsche warned us that what we call something may be
considerably more important that what it is. This is as true now as it was a
century ago. Speaking even more directly to our time, Martin Heidegger
(1889-1963) reaffirmed Nietzsche's observations about naming, in his work
What Is Called Thinking [Heidegger 1968:161]. In the process of thinking
about something, Heidegger wrote the first and most elemental "act of theory"
is to define each thing with a definite name, that is, to declare that "X is
Y."Addressing some of the vagueness in modern diplomatic history, Bruce
Cumings comments in more detail on this phenomenon. By naming–the

simple process of attaching a name to an event–the memory creates a location for the idea and determines how it can be recalled through the comparison of established "categories of thought" [Cumings 1993: 541].

When we name something, we release it from the general and abstract field of the present. We provide a flag by which the event can be identified even as the details and sharper memories of the occasion fade into the past. The flag is the means by which we separate specific events from other, undefined, experience. A name makes it possible to identify an event in the context of other events, by both linking the commonality and affirming the uniqueness. In the process of remembering that an event is a "war," we separate it from memories of "conflicts" or "parties." Once our minds find the proper category, the process is to identify its distinctiveness, by contrast to other items or events in that category. When we grope for the name of a past acquaintance, we know that we are more likely to recall it if we can locate its owner in time and space. We are also aware that once the name is recalled it is much easier to identify other individuals, their recollection stimulated by the shared location or time.

The fighting in Korea has been identified in so many ways that it is possible to argue that it has never been identified at all. Each identity results from the understanding available to the person who identified it; those involved called it many things. Lt. Gen. Matthew B. Ridgway was probably the first to use "forgotten war," an identity that has caught on. But it is always necessary to add "the Korean War," because in a sense we have forgotten what it is that we forgot.

Robert Oliver's definition of the event as "the war nobody wanted" is equally disturbing, and it may well be very insightful. Other interesting titles have been adopted; each tells us something of the views of the person selecting it. Among such definitions/identities are "Mr. Truman's folly," the "wrong war," the "Communist war," the "Asian war," the "unknown war," the "empathetic War," the "war that never was," the "war before Vietnam." Not to be outdone, this book will suggest a new identification: "the ignored war."

Returning to Friedrich Nietzsche for a moment, it is worth pursuing the connection he made between the lack of a name and the lack of historical characterization. He calls this phenomena *historica abscondita*, the absence of a historical period from the memory of a people or a nation. Nietzsche's phrase refers to a national event that is missing from the chronological and subject memory. It could even be translated as "secreting" or even as "theft" of history.

A contemporary historian, Pierre Machetrey, refers to this same phenomenon as "structured absence." He suggests that memory can be organized in such a way that it will eventually alter other memories, or leave memories out. People do this all the time. That is, they choose a narrative of their lives that allows some things–usually events they prefer not to remember–to fade away. This can create a difficulty within a person's self-concept that, at the extreme, requires professional help to work out.

The problem with structuring memory in order to avoid things is that one must still must   live with the effects of the event. Persons often find themselves having to deal with ideas, thoughts, emotions, or events that result from something they simply do not recall. Thus their response is based on a misconception and is very likely not to accomplish what it attempts.

A simple illustration may help clarify this idea. Suppose you are hit in the eye by a bully at the local beach. The eye turns black and blue. Because you are embarrassed, when asked about the black eye you say it was an accident: while you were at the beach, you tripped and fell and hit your face on a rock. Years later, walking along the beach, you discover yourself carefully avoiding the rocks–but unfortunately, you are not on the lookout for bullies. Your mind retains the effect of the event, but your structured memory denies you the tools by which you might otherwise deal more successfully with the experience. The Korean War is simply not a part of our collective memory, nor is it a part of how we explain the present, even though it still greatly influence us.

Interestingly, it was the lack of a specific name that made it possible at the time for the Korean War to be fought with any sense of legitimacy. The American constitution gives the Congress the power to declare war. President Truman's identification of America's involvement in Korea as a "police action" took it out of the realm of congressional authority–at least, there was precedent for that view. America had done it several times before. This "nonwar"definition allowed President Truman to commit the American people to fighting in Korea without consultation with or the approval of the legislative branch.

When Harry Truman first defined the action as a "police action," he put himself in a position to claim that we were not at war. A police action is not a war–not even a conflict. It could easily be written off as just one more occasion America was doing its "housekeeping" chores. By downplaying the event, whether this was his intention or not, Truman reduced the significance of what was taking place in Korea in the minds of those for whom the term "police action" had little meaning. President Truman was to use this phrase until November 2, 1952. By that date the dead and wounded in Korea were being counted in the thousands.

Not only did Truman's attitude belittle what was being done, but it provided grounds for ridiculing his own approach. Michael Pearlman, of the U.S. Army Command and Staff College has suggested that General MacArthur did just that when he said, "Even if Truman was not waging war against Red China, China was certainly waging war against the United States" [Pearlman:289].

The Korean War is often identified as little more than an unfortunate side effect of the U.S. new role in world leadership. In the Truman administration this was especially true, since the conflict was being conducted under the banner of the United Nations. For some the connection provided identification but little more; Secretary of State Dean Acheson would call the United Nations "window dressing" [as quoted in Pearlman:283]. It was to President Truman's advantage–and in fairness to him, probably to America's long-term advantage–to keep the fighting in Korea as low key as possible. Nevertheless, this early failure to identify the event was the first of many reasons why the Korean War has dropped so far back in the American memory. It was not until many years later, as direct memories of it were already vanishing, that the event in Korea in the early 1950s was acknowledged to have been a war.

As suggested earlier, the pattern suggested by "structured absence" is not simply lack of interest, or the diminishing of old events. While it is sometimes the result of active, even aggressive, efforts designed to repress a memory, it is not necessarily the result of some evil intent. Nor does it require action by someone in authority or the power of a careful conspiracy to make the *decision* to downgrade a memory. Rather the condition of structured absence results from a far less sinister, but equally disastrous, failure to take an event seriously. The Korean War is poorly remembered by Americans because they do not take it seriously.

Another aspect of the phenomenon of naming is the intimate relationship that exists between how a war is thought of and how it was fought. In retrospect, several decisions during the Korean War determined that the war would be difficult to remember. These were at the time seemingly significant and well-considered actions by persons in authority. Two or three illustrations might make this more clearer.

Consider for a moment the disposition and identification of the bodies of Americans who died in this struggle. For the first time in our national history, the killed in action were returned for burial to the United States. The reason was basic: the nation's leadership had no confidence in the outcome of the war. From the beginning, they did not believe that they could maintain unrestricted access to American cemeteries in Korea. America's dead were brought home because the military were not sure the ultimate goal of their involvement–an occupied and united Korean nation–could be realized [Piehler 1995:20].

The effect of this decision was compounded by the implications of a second one. The military and civilian authorities responsible for the internment of the dead decided that those buried in national cemeteries would be identified only by name, rank, and date of birth. The markers for those who died in Korea would not state where or why they had given their lives.

For more than a year after this first became known, the families of several of these American casualties voiced their objection. They felt the decision was unfair and insensitive. They understandably believed that it was only right that the graves of their loved ones be identified by the cause in which they had died. Finally, in 1951, the secretary of the army responded to these concerns, but he still felt the phrase "Korean War" was inappropriate; it was also, at that time, inaccurate. The final agreement was that the graves of those killed in the Korean War would be marked simply "Korea."

The question of identification arose again during the planning and construction of the Korean War Veterans Memorial in Washington, D.C. Many, including the leaders and members of the Korean War Veterans Association, expressed serious reservations about the design. They asked that the memorial include a permanent listing of the dead, engraved in an appropriate place on one of the walls. The Memorial Commission deliberately blocked the idea. The concern of the authorities, which they managed to articulate to a rather large audience, was that to list the names would give the impression those who had died in Korea were "victims" [Piehler 1995:178]. There was another reason the names were not listed, one as widely discussed. It had to do with the fact that even as the monument was being built and dedicated, American servicemen were still dying in the Korean War.

The Korean War does not suffer in South Korea from the effects of structured absence. Unlike in America, a strong memory of the Korean War has been an essential part of the tradition by which the people of the Republic of South Korea have preserved their identity. In contrast to the American response, the South Korean government has made remarkable efforts to memorialize the war. At the same time, they have made a major effort to acknowledge the contribution made by the United States and the United Nations, in the preservation of their country.

South Korea has established several memorials. A statue to General Douglas MacArthur, whom they remember with considerable affection, has been constructed at the harbor at Inchon, the scene of his greatest success. It was MacArthur, they believe, who stopped the invasion and returned the capital of Seoul to them in September 1950. In 1977 the Republic of South Korea constructed a memorial at Paju to honor the four services of the American contingent involved in the struggle. The memorial includes a series of bronze reliefs illustrating some of the major battles. Each of the fifty states that sent troops to fight in Korea is represented by state flags. At Pusan, in 1980, the Koreans have erected a monument in honor of the heroic defense oft the "Pusan perimeter."

THE RESPONSE TO VETERANS

Another way in which naming has affected the memory of the Korean War is reflected in the veterans' understanding of it. The returning Korean veteran did not experience the rejection suffered by many who returned from Vietnam; rather, the Korean veteran experienced something akin to indifference. No one seemed to notice that they had been gone, what they had done, or that they had returned.

Unlike during World War II, those on the home front were not greatly affected by the war. Few really understood the extent to which America was involved. The war effort produced none of the shortages experienced during World War II; there was no rationing, there were no restrictions on travel, the freeze on housing was nearly over, and gas was readily available. New cars were being produced, and an increasing number of persons had the money to buy them. Since the war did little to disturb the life of the average American, few were aware of the coming and going of soldiers or of the events which took them away and brought them home. This lack of interest was compounded: the longer the war continued, the less interest it held for citizens. Because military personnel were rotated on an individual basis during the Korean War, they left and returned as a steady but uneventful stream of individuals.

It did not take long before the Korean veteran began to recognize that the situation was considerably different for them than it had been for those returning home earlier. It would be more correct, perhaps, to suggest that it did not take long before Korean veterans began to *reflect,* rather than acknowledge, the manner in which they were treated. There was little said during this time; the norm was a quiet acceptance. They had gone when called, and they had—most of them— returned. The nation did not consider it a major event when they left, and no one considered it one when they returned. To some degree it became less important even to the veterans.

Some have identified this sense of unreality as apathy. But apathy is too powerful a term. While it sounds paradoxical, the term has come to mean more than just "lack of interest or response"; it has taken on a more aggressive tone. What the veteran experienced was not so much a lack of interest, as it was (and is) a reluctance to call attention to themselves or their contribution. The phrase that comes to mind from this period in American history is "no big deal."

One way to illustrate the veteran's low-key response is to look at the use of postwar benefits. It is true that the GI benefits available to Korean veterans were not as wide or as grand as those available after World War II. More helpful to our understanding of the veteran's self-image, however, is to the very small percentage of the Korean War veterans who took advantage of the benefits offered. The veterans were themselves not inclined to be affirming of the Korean War or their part in it. This was the same situation in which the larger public found itself as well.

In their excellent book *The Wages of War* [Severo 1997], Richard Severo and Lewis Milford provide a meaningful look at the Korean veteran. They identify the veterans as disquieting, machinelike products of their special times. This condition, which the authors describe, is reflected in the veteran's almost drug like disinterest. The word "ashamed" is too strong, but the Korea veterans' unfocused discounting of their parts in the war and its place in history is a disturbing contrast to the assertive individualism of the veterans of World War II [Severo 1997:327].

This indifference is almost a by-product of the idea of memory. It requires us to look at two other questions. The first has to do with why the Korean War has been ignored, or forgotten, to the extent that it has. This question concerns the *reasons why* Americans have chosen to, or have been allowed to, forget the war.

This question of reason is in contrast to the second question, which asks; what are the *events or nonevents* that explain why the Korean War has been so forgotten? At first this may appear far too subtle a distinction, but it will help if we address the first question as having to do with *why* and the second question as dealing with *how*. The first should address the purpose, whether conscious or unconscious, for forgetting. The second asks what conditions have contributed to the rather insignificant role the Korean War plays in the national memory.

Part of the answer to the first question is America's natural ambivalence toward war. Despite the fact that Americans are as violent as other people, the nation has never supported the militance that many nations take for granted. When we are at peace, we seem to forget war and what it takes to fight them. Only in the post-Korea era has America given proper attention to being prepared. Historically, America entered war with an almost criminal lack of preparation. The nation, perhaps due to confidence in its own ability, maintained a sort of naive optimism, assuming there was little need to prepare for war until it arrived.

A second consideration in this question of *why* is the fact that American forces in Korea were prevented from winning—both by a powerful enemy and by political maneuvering. They were beaten and then held in check by a strong "peasant" army. It was an enemy many had assumed to be inferior and that was fighting for a cause that westerners considered invalid. How could people be ultimately committed to communism?

Politically, the United Nations forces—and by that we mean primarily American Forces—were put into a defensive mode that denied them the advantage of aggressive action. When the inevitable happened and a stalemate resulted, American servicemen were blamed as if for defeat. The lack of an American victory, whatever the political implication, was attributed to weakness on the part of those fighting the war. The result was, many believed, unacceptable; certainly it was not what Americans had come to expect. It was not what the great victory of World War II had promised them. As a sad contrast to the euphoric high of the "good war," this less than ideal effort in Korea was best forgotten.

The people of America were strangely willing to accept the idea that Korea was a major defeat. Lacking some other explanation, it was easy to lay a good portion of the responsibility at the feet of the young men and women who had carried the burden of the war in Korea. Needing someone to blame for what seemed a national disgrace, the American people turned their anger against the military, identifying the armed forces as the weak link.

The United States had won so significantly in Europe and the Pacific, and lost so disgracefully in Korea; many concluded the differences had to be that the young men and women now in the military were inferior. Soon the nation, and the military itself, turned on its own fighting forces. The charges against them included a lack of physical and moral strength, and of the characteristic that made Americans great–gumption. According to this view, the failure to achieve victory in Korea could be traced to a general weakening of the American character, encouraged, if not brought on, by the "liberal education" of the young.

The unforgivable thing is that the military, particularly the U. S. Army, turned on its own. Brig. Gen. Samuel L. A. Marshall, a fine historian and author of one of the better Korean War books, *Pork Chop Hill* [Marshall 1986], would accuse the army, as well as the nation, of besmirching its own people. Americans, he said, having no other immediate explanation, had cast aspersions on the fine "young men and women who had nothing to do with either the design of the war or its outcome" [Severo 1997:344].

It is only fair to remember that during this time the U. S. Army was having its own troubles. Sen. Joseph McCarthy was launching his crusade against the "communists in olive-drab." The military was not in a good position to defend what had happened in Korea, even though it had not been to blame for it. The smear campaign directed against the military was supported by no less an organization than the American Legion. The Legion, full of World War II veterans, felt that the pride of its members had been challenged; the great victory they had won was somehow besmirched by the failure to win victory in Korea. They were willing to assume that the less-than-loyal Korea veterans were "soft on communism." America's new fighting men and women, the old veterans suggested, had failed to carry on the strong traditions and high moral principals of the American soldier.

Yet another response to the question *why* may be found in the fact that for the first time in our history, Americans prisoners of war were compromised. Though the prisoner of war percentage in Korea was about the same as in other wars, Americans in the 1950s considered the number disproportionate. These unfortunate men were painted with the dark designation of disloyalty, tarred with the brush of treason, simply because they had been captured. As never before, Americans who had been captured were considered disloyal. Just being captured was considered sign of weakness, of unwillingness to fight for America, as seen as evidence that the servicemen and women had fallen short of the "historical standards of honor, character, loyalty, courage, and personal integrity" [Severo 1997:344]. America, in its fear and misunderstanding, assumed that all prisoners had been brainwashed. Having little if any understanding of what the term "brainwashing" meant, many Americans thought they had something to fear from those who were released. The POW was viewed with considerable suspicion.

Though the prisoner of war count in Korea was about the same percentage as in other wars, Americans, in the 1950s, considered the numbers outlandish.

Just being captured was taken as evidence that the servicemen and women had fallen short of the "historical standards of honor, character, loyalty, courage, and personal integrity." [Severo 1997:344]

Maj. William Mayer, the source of the above quote concerning "historical standards," was a military investigator who seemed determined to prove that the American soldier was weak. "Fully one third of all Americans captured in Korea," he said "gave in when the communists subjected them to brainwashing." The source of this information is not cited, and further, exhaustive study suggests that it not true. But it was quickly adopted by those seeking an answer, and it was followed by accusations that the nation at large had become increasingly weak. It seemed to follow, if one accepted this line of thought, that we had something to fear from returning prisoners of war, that they should be watched–as a result of their brainwashing by the Communist Chinese, they were prone to "communist tendencies."

Once the scapegoat was identified, nearly everyone joined the crusade. The outspoken Betty Friedan, in a statement rich in irony, wrote that the young men of America had been made passive by mothers who were "apathetic, dependent, infantile, purposeless [and] shockingly non-human." Dr. Benjamin Spock, the great guru of American parents, and a man who had no reluctance to speak his mind, said that the American young people were "undisciplined, over coddled." The ultra-American director of the Federal Bureau of Investigation, J. Edgar Hoover, complained about the "softness of American young people." Such weakness was unacceptable in light of the great danger of "communist subversion." Even Adm. Hyman Rickover, a technologically progressive military leader but somewhat illiberal commentator, lent his powerful voice to those focusing on the Korean veteran. He suggested that it was "relatively easy to confuse our [troops]," because they had [Severo 1997:344].

Conservatives and liberals appeared to form an unholy alliance in their willingness to assume an American failure in Korea. Though they approached it from different directions, both schools were willing to agree that the young Americans who had fought were of flawed character and that some were attracted to communism. This attraction, it was felt, reflected the general disarray of American education and evidenced a tremendous diminution of the "American people's spirit of devotion to a common cause"[Severo 1997:344].

Twenty-one United Nations prisoners of war decided to remain in the hands of their communist captors. Of the thousands held, this was hardly a significant percentage, but their failure to return underscored the great fear Americans were experiencing of the idea of mind control. Perhaps this fear is best illustrated in the postwar movie *The Manchurian Candidate* (1962), with Frank Sinatra and Angela Lansbury. The movie, which has gained acceptance as a classic, was not that good, but it touched the American attitude about brainwashing. In the years after the Korean War, Americans were bombarded with the idea that brainwashed soldiers and sailors could be programmed, like sleeping robots, to rise against their own people.

Hindsight allows us to realize that this was neither true nor even possible. The Communists were not that successful brainwashing prisoners. The success they had was in the area of political conditioning, not in the "re-programming" of the personalities of captives. But the image of young men giving in to the harshness of prison and the indoctrination of Marxist thought is clearly associated with the Korean War. It has proven difficult to overcome.

THE QUESTION OF HOW

The second question to be considered has to do with *how* the loss of memory occurred. Americans have allowed the memory of the Korean War to fade from their historical consciousness. It is only in the last few years that much progress has been made in the effort to include the Korean War in national celebration and commemoration. In looking for an answer to the question of *how* the Korean War has been forgotten, one easy possibility is the timing of the event. After the very popular and well-defined goals of World War II, and the awesome domestic discontent of Vietnam, Americans had much else on their minds. As Robert Mitcham's character says to Mai Britt, in the movie *The Hunters* (1953), "Korea came along too soon after the really big one. It is hard to sell anyone on it."

In fact, no one was selling it at all. The media coverage produced for home consumption was different from that during World War II, and different, as well, from the extremes of media coverage in Vietnam. Press releases during the Korean War tended to express general support for the war but a rather hearty disapproval of the military and administrative conduct of it. The difference, for the American people, was that the press did not challenge the American purpose. Press coverage, particularly in periodicals, merely drew the public's attention to the confusion and lack of identifiable goals.

While there was television coverage of the Korean War, that medium was still in its childhood; it was not found in the average American home. For those who had television, the footage provided by the networks was primarily used to illustrate the news commentary. That is, the film served as background for voice-overs. It did not bring the war into the homes as would be the case for Vietnam. For those at home, the primary coverage was in newspapers, radio, and periodicals. By some internal standard or unexpressed agreement, the majority of the pictures of the Korean War were images of personal defeat, sorrow, and fear, but few showed actual destruction. There were few pictures released of bleeding bodies and failed missions [Moeller 1991:280-286].

Returning to the question of naming, there is much to be learned about the failure of memory for the Korean War in how the United States has commemorated that war. Consider for a moment the naming of the great conflict that divided the American people in the mid-1860s. When it came time to collect the thousands of documents of this period, the official name given to the archival collection was, *The Official Records of the War of the Rebellion*. But the conflict was seen as variously the Civil War, the War between the States, the War of the Confederacy, or the war between the blue and the gray. In the programs designed to commemorate the war, however, every effort was made by the federal Monument and Battlefield Commission to ease the wounds of the divided nation by encouraging monuments to Americans on both sides of the conflict.

During the last few years there has been a growing interest in the idea of commemoration. One of the finest books on this issue is John Bodnar's *Remaking America: Public Memory, Commemoration, and Patriotism in the Twentieth Century* [Bodnar 1996]. Beginning with a discussion of the Vietnam Veterans Memorial and the long road that led to its construction, Bodnar looks at the attitude reflected by the long wait for commemoration. The difficulty with Vietnam lay in the fact few divide the question of the war from that of its veterans; the politics of the one was the politics of the other.

PUBLIC MEMORY

"Public memory emerges from the intersection of official and vernacular cultural expressions. The former originates in the concerns of cultural leaders or authorities at all levels. . . . [The] vernacular culture, on the other hand, represents an array of specialized interests that are grounded in parts of the whole" [Moeller 1999:280-286]. Another way of saying this is that persons in authority and responsibility often believe it is important to commemorate political values rather than military events. That is, they pay tribute to the beliefs and values that led the nation to war rather than to the conflict itself. In contrast, the average American is interested in recording the events as they knew and lived them. The participants, in this case the Korean veterans, were interested in a memorial to those who served. Thus it is often the case that planning a commemoration of a significant historical event is itself a controversy of some significance.

Who are these "responsible people?" Who are the "they" of this particular scenario? They are not some evil group, determined to misrepresent history, but rather the cultural leaders of the society. It is a fairly large group from the professions, business middle management, government, the military, small (but vocal) businessmen, and local political leaders. Its members are usually "movers and shakers." What they want is the continuation of the systems and political structures they have. What they do is lend their position and power to the commemoration of values that maintain their positions. They are interested in preventing social unrest over or disillusionment in the practical, programmed political behavior of the community.

The vernacular is represented by what Bodnar identified as the "ordinary people," basically indifferent to political and patriotic messages. They are civic minded, but that they are more in a tune with, and interested in, the preservation of personal memories. The event being remembered played a significant part in their lives, and they in it. These personal memories are related to, but considerably different from, either civil or social values. In many cases the value involved is little more than autobiographical for those participating. In the case of a war, this group will include those who served and those for whom the community's involvement was of personal significance. Thus, the veteran and those seeking community attachment are after some way in which they can connect to an event that the community considers important.

In the final analysis, however, though representatives of all three groups will be represented–that is, cultural leader, veteran, and the vernacular–the source of the money and the power will most likely have the final say. What is commemorated will be more inclined to espouse the role of "citizen duties over citizen rights"[Bodnar 1996:19]. This is the role the community sees as most important.

One of the interesting characteristics of what is often called the "postmodern age" is the continuing effort to create a new symbolism for participation in the American tradition–not only new symbolisms, but also the desire to develop new ways to understand and express this same tradition. This has not yet been successful. So, in the absence of new myths to acknowledge the event, the memory of the Korean War is still dependent on how well the images of the public–vernacular and participant–can overcome the more narrow agenda of the cultural memory [Bodnar 1996:252]. So far, the vernacular is the more powerful weight on this balance.

The personal experiences of those involved in a major event are often better preserved in literature than in a memorial. In the long run, it can be argued that it is not the lack of memorials that have led to a lack of appreciation for the Korean War. It is more likely that "ordinary people" lack either an understanding of, or appreciation for, the war. This lack of appreciation is fed by the silence (absence of) in literature on the period. It is interesting to note that even in Bodnar's excellent book, which considers commemorative events from the sailing of the *Mayflower* to the Gulf War, there is little discussion of remembering the Korean War. There is no index entry for the Korean War at all.

The term *war* carries with it a whole set of implications. It suggests a goal, and it identifies a degree of commitment and investment–or at least it did in the 1950s. Most certainly, at that time, the terms *conflict* and *action* carry different implications. The fact is, the United States did not really know what it was getting involved ind when they sent troops. Nor did it ever establish primary goals they expected to fulfill as a result of their involvement. It did not really define what it was that young people were dying for. The long silence since then has sustained that lack of proper identification. That, and our confusion as to the outcome, has left our memory of the war without legitimacy or justification.

Chapter 4

Who Is To Blame

Misconceptions, miscalculation, and confusion were prominent,
perhaps dominant features of the policy process on both sides.

Michael Hunt

Kim Il Sung, the premier of North Korea and once a battalion commander in
the Soviet Far East forces, sent his troops across the 38th Parallel on June 25,
1950. In doing so he took upon himself much of the blame for starting the
Korean War. It is hard to argue with the approximately one hundred thousand
troops, ninety planes, and more than 144 Russian-built T-34 medium tanks
that appeared on the frontier. But it is not that simple.

Who started the Korean War? If one means only what nation's troops first
crossed a neighbor's border, the question can be answered with certainty. The
answer is the Democratic People's Republic of Korea. But if one means who
is responsible for allowing (or pushing) events to the point of war, the answer
is more complex. The answer includes both the accumulation of facts and a
look at differing points of view. So while determining blame may be difficult,
it is nevertheless important to look at what happened. The causes are
understandably seen differently by different people and have altered
considerably with the passage of time. Unfortunately, the Korean War was the
result of complex causes, and the blame probably needs to be spread around.

Orthodox American historiographies suggest the Korean War was the
outcome of international communist aggression. When South Korea was first
invaded, many were inclined to believe it was a diversion set up by the Soviet
premier, Joseph Stalin, to draw attention from a war to be launched in Europe.
The "diversion theory" has proven to be inaccurate, but the belief continues
that the invasion somehow fit into the larger Communist desire to rule the
world. There were divergent views, of course. Some blamed the Communist
Chinese; others, like I. F. Stone, were more or less sure that the war was the
result of South Korean provocations, supported by the Americans and carried
out by President Syngman Rhee.

It is fairly well accepted that Kim Il Sung initiated the war with South Korea to unify the Korean nation under a single government. It is also largely proven that Kim Il Sung came to his decision after consultation with Stalin and Mao Tse-tung. In these discussions Stalin provided some encouragement and promised to provide aid, both supplies and air power [Dong-A 1971:44].

China calls the war in Korea *Kamgmei Yuanchao Yungdon*–loosely the "Movement to Resist American Aid to Korea." The blame, from this perspective, is to be laid on the U. S. imperialism: in contrast, American Sen. Robert Taft blamed the war on the wishyewashyness in the State Department and its lack of a China policy. Maj. Gen. Lewis B. Hershey, director of the U. S. Selective Service, blamed the failure on the absence of a strong foreign policy, of which Korea was but one example. John Kennedy blamed the lack of a well-conceived foreign policy on America's past presidents. The American Legion identified the American Civil Liberties Union as the prime culprit. The folks at home tended to blame the war on the nasty commies [Severo 1997:21].

The truth probably lies somewhere else, and if properly understood, it is more complex. The military actions are more easily traced, but considerable work remains if we are to ever understand the political, economic, even psychological reasons that set this force in motion. New materials that have surfaced during the 1980s and 1990s that help in this inquiry.

THE DEMOCRATIC PEOPLE'S REPUBLIC OF NORTH KOREA

The American view is that the Democratic People's Republic attacked the Republic of Korea "without provocation." When the Soviet occupation forces pulled out from North Korea, they left behind a powerful indigenous force, the North Korean People's Army (NKPA). (Its Korean name *In Min Gun)*. The NKPA was a strong, well-trained, mobile, force and was equipped with both defensive and offensive weapons. From the first of the year, 1950, it had been involved in a series of border incidents. Over the first six months incidents increased in both number and intensity; then, in May 1950, the raids dropped to almost nothing. North Korean civilians along the border were evacuated, generally during the night. The railroad running north from Kaesong to Pyongyang was removed in secret. In early June, North Korean radio began a series of broadcasts pushing for the unification of Korea. The number of broadcasts beamed into South Korea increased and their central theme was the idea that unification might be accomplished by peaceful means.

These signs were not taken as seriously as they might have been, but neither were they totally ignored. At military headquarters in Washington, D.C., March 1950, an investigation was conducted. As a part of the review, Maj. Gen. Charles A. Willoughby, the G-2 (intelligence) officer on the staff of General MacArthur, Supreme Commander, Allied Powers, in Japan, cabled the Pentagon that the North Korean raids would probably continue, but "there will be no civil war in Korea this spring or summer." Even the newly operating

Central Intelligence Agency agreed that a North Korean invasion was possible but that its "launching in the summer of 1950 did not appear imminent" [Blair 1987:58].

However, on June 25, 1950, the North Korean leaders sent their assembled troops into battle. The plan was to strike hard, push quickly, and eradicate South Korea in a campaign lasting no more than five days. To acknowledge the attack as another stage in a civil war that had existed since the liberation of Korea in 1945 helps explain this projection. Kim Il Sung was sure the people of South Korea would rise up and support the advancing troops. He was determined to unite Korea under the control of the Democratic People's Republic.

It is easy to look at the situation and conclude that North Korea was a puppet of either the Soviet Union or international communism. Many others, of course, maintain the invasion was the product of a clash between Russia and the United States.

THE SOVIET UNION

For a long time, the conventional American wisdom was that the Korean War was a phase in the Soviet agenda of expansion, a view suggested by Chul Soh Jin [Jin 1963]. The Soviet Union was America's enemy of choice, and since the end of World War II the United States had tended to blame what it could on the "Reds." Most Americans believed it was only a manner of time until the long-feared Russian effort at world conquest broke out.

Despite these fears there are many reasons to believe Joseph Stalin was not anxious to support North Korea in its invasion of South Korea. It was not time. The premier, however, apparently changed his mind in early 1950, perceiving a weakness in the position of the Truman administration. Stalin became convinced the United States did not have the will to get involved in a major war in Asia [Summers 1996:7].

Stalin's view seems to have been based on a series of observations. One was the Communist victory in the Chinese civil war. The fact that the United States had deserted Nationalist China at the last moment suggested to Stalin that it would defend South Korea. The Soviets also had freed themselves from nuclear blackmail, when they tested its own atomic bomb shortly before the Korean War began. Also, Moscow was very aware of the drastic cuts in the American military budget and the resulting decline in its military posture.

While it was probably not a major reason for Soviet involvement, the situation became more complex when Dean Acheson, Secretary of State, made his January 1950 statement suggesting that Korea fell outside the area of American concern. If nothing else, the speech suggested that the United States had a poor understanding of the world situation. Michael Pearlman argues, "Not wanting to test U. S. resolve, let alone wage war against the West, he [Stalin] approved Kim Il Sung's invasion only because it promised to be a quick victory in a location Americans discounted and would not defend"

[Pearlman 1999:288].

The Soviet Union was quick to blame the United States and Syngman Rhee–as well as the United Nations–for the outbreak of war. The Soviet encyclopedia puts it this way:

In summer of 1950, American imperialists shifted from preparing aggression to direct acts of aggression. On June 25 ten divisions of Syngman Rhee's troops concentrated on the 38th Parallel attacked North Korean by order of General MacArthur, commander of American troops in the Far East [as quoted in Merrill 1989:191]

Perhaps more interesting is the suggestion that the pressure for the attack for and the eventual Chinese involvement, was part of a larger Soviet agenda designed to place the United States and China in an irreconcilable conflict.

CONSPIRACY THEORIES

Conspiracy theories always rise up to explain the historically unexplained. Certainly the outbreak of the Korean War has its own set of theories. The term "conspiracy" is used here to mean a mutual agreement among nations, or individuals, to create some action or event. Some of these ideas are still taken seriously.

One of the more persistent suggestions is that the United States and the Republic of Korea collaborated to entrap the North Koreans into military action. This theory is brought to us by the same people who charge President Roosevelt for engineering the attack on Pearl Harbor. America, the theory goes, always reacts better when being attacked, than when on the attack. The point of this action was twofold, servicing the needs of both nations. It would allow the United States to establish a permanent imperial base in Korea, and for South Korea, the aggression would guarantee the continuation of the weak government of Syngman Rhee.

A second scenario suggests that the Soviet Union, North Korea, and Communist China conspired to begin a war in Asia. Robert Simmons, in *The Strained Alliance: Peking, P'yongyang, Moscow and the Politics of the Civil War* [Simmons 1975], argues that if they were not actually planning a war together, they certainly conspired to enable the war to occur.

Closely linked with this is a related conspiracy of which one of the more outspoken proponents is Lloyd C. Gardner, in *The Korean War* [Gardner 1968]. He asserts that the North Korean invasion of South Korea was the opening move in a Communist offensive for worldwide domination. However, while it is fairly certain that Premier Mao Tse-tung and Stalin were both aware of North Korea's decision to invade, there is less evidence that the nations involved were acting under the aegis of international communism. In fact, failure to understand the difference between national and international communism is a significant part of the inability of the United Nations to comprehend the depth of the problem it faced.

The actual element of conspiracy, if there was one, may have been in the willingness of major political powers to use small and vulnerable nations in the Cold War. That is, the Korean War may simply have been a convenient battleground for one more clash between nations who did not have the courage to take on each other openly.

There was also, of course, the United Nations theory, which held that the Korean War was a part of Harry Truman's plot to establish the authority of the United Nations as an international body able to interfere in the affairs of independent nations.

While not so much a conspiracy as an alterative source of blame, the whole question of civil conflict must also be considered. Since the liberation of Korea in 1945, strong nationalistic feelings had dominated the political systems of both sections of the nation. These feelings were strong enough to have brought "southerners" to Pyongyang and Haeju for discussions of national unity. One result of these conferences was the creation of the Korean Worker's Party by a merger of the existing communist parties of the North and the South.

Rhee, the aging president of South Korea, was probably more committed to unification than anyone else, but he operated from a condition of weakness. It was therefore necessary for him to use every possible weapon at his disposal to maintain the security of his nation. It is reasonable to assume that he would also use any means he could to bring about the unification of the Korean nation. Thus military action in Korea might be identified as American–or UN–interference in a conflict emerging from the vast political and class upheaval in Korea and in China. This possibility is yet to be completely understood.

THE PEOPLE'S REPUBLIC OF CHINA

Many believe that Communist China was the primary enemy in the Korean War. Some still hold that it was partially responsible for the outbreak of war in Korea in 1950. But the question of China's involvement is really two questions. Both may well relate to Chinese national identity. In the past few years, new materials have become available that while reflecting the complexity of the situation, make it easier to understand what happened. Red China, while communist, most likely entered the Korean War less as an act of aggression than in response to a perceived threat to Chinese security. To look at the question of China's role, it is necessary first to examine its involvement in the North Korean decision to invade, then to address Communist China's entry into the fighting in 1950.

Certainly Beijing knew Kim Il Sung was up to something. Very likely Mao Tse-tung and Stalin discussed the possibility of war several times between December 1949 and February 1950. It is likely as well that Mao and Kim Il Sung had some conversations concerning the invasion.

Whatever his involvement in the invasion itself, it is clear that Mao worked closely with Kim to repatriate the more than a hundred thousand Korean troops and their equipment which in 1950 were still on Chinese soil. These volunteers had fought under Mao during the Chinese civil war. But other than these arrangements, it is important to note how limited was the military aid China provided the North Koreans during the early phase of the war.

Chairman Mao was moving cautiously along two parallel paths. One was Red China's need for continued good relations with Stalin. This was expressed in Mao's discussion with Stalin of his plan to enter Korea, in a defensive posture. The more important question concerns China's entry into the war late in 1950. Records indicate that when the United Nations began moving across the 38th Parallel, and threatened to wipe out the NKPA, Stalin urged Mao to go to the aid of Kim Il Sung's collapsing forces. The Chinese felt a sense of duty to come to the aid of their communist neighbors and to support the revolutionary spirit around the world. The Chinese were also aware of the significance of North Korea in their own security. Mao Tse-tung was not immune to the appeal of international communism with China at the center.

We are aware that when Mao met with Stalin in Moscow, there was a suggestion of Soviet air support. It appears that at this point Mao refused to become involved; he suggested instead that North Koreans revert to guerrilla warfare. But under pressure, and in response to promises of aid–particularly air cover–Mao agreed. China would enter the war. On October 4 Mao ordered the Chinese People's Volunteers into action. The Communist Chinese forces (CCF) consisted of two army groups, comprising nine corps-sized field armies, with thirty infantry divisions, a total of about 380,000 men. The CCF XIII Army Group faced the U. S. Eighth Army, and CCF IX Army Group was to move across from U. S. X Corps.

The second path Mao followed had to do with China's economic structure and the needs of his new revolutionary government. Mao was justly afraid that a prolonged struggle with the United States would damage the economic reconstruction he had been trying to produce and weaken the stability established since the revolution.

According to Marshal Nie Rongzhen, the acting chief of staff of the People's Liberation Army in 1950, the majority opinion among those in civilian and military leadership was that a war should not be fought "unless absolutely necessary." The war to "resist America and aid Korea," was also opposed by Chinese military leader Marshal Lin Piao, who rejected an offer of command of the Chinese People's Volunteers. As more Soviet documents become available, it is increasingly apparent that many members of the Chinese Communist Party, including the army commander and the foreign minister, did not want to go to war with America over Korea. The idea of volunteers was suggested as a means of avoiding any official involvement or a declaration of war. Even on the eve of the Chinese entrance into the war, Marshall Peng The-huai, the commander, briefed his subordinate commanders. "We do not want to fight a major war. Nor do we intend to declare war on America, but only to assist Korean revolutionary war in the name of People's Volunteers" [Yu

1998:6].

Following the United Nations success at Inchon in late September, Chinese officers were sent into Korea to prepare for the intervention. What was lacking was a date. On June 30, 1950, the Chinese sent advanced parties into Korea, and ten days later the Military Affairs Committee recommended the organization of forces to defend their border. At this point there was the willingness to send troops if necessary to help the North Koreans. There continued to be concern among Mao's colleagues, but by October 2, 1950, the decision had basically been made.

On October 8, as the result of a meeting between Mao and Kim Il Sung at Beijing, Peng The-huai was placed at the head of a joint Chinese-Korean command. There is still some difference of opinion about who was the Chinese commander. Clay Blair and John Soulden say it was Lin Bao, while Michael Hunt suggests Peng The-huai. Despite concern over the limited air support available, the rapid advance of American troops made it necessary to make a decision. Finally Mao set October 19 for the major crossing of the Yalu.

So why did Red China send troops into North Korea in October and November 1950? The reason was the overwhelming "domestic preoccupations of Chinese leaders on the eve of the Korean War and the stress from what was seen as a compelling threat to China's security" [Foot 1991:417]. It is difficult to determine to what extent Mao's arguments reflected his agenda or were simply offered to convince dissenters. But there is little doubt that he was supportive–at least to some degree–of China's duty as an international communist body to rescue its Korean neighbor, to help maintain the revolutionary spirit around the world.

But more than this, Mao was greatly concerned about the possibility of American action against China itself. Mao, it appears, was convinced that military intervention was necessary to prevent the enemy from dominating the Yalu River and thus posing a constant threat to the northeast of the nation. But China's entry was also needed to provide the fleeing North Koreans a secure base of operations. Further, Mao was interested in denying an imperialist victory that would fan counterrevolutionary sentiments in China; the premier was concerned about the reactionary influence in his country of the Americans. Michael H. Hunt sees China's mobilization as a chance to involve the "urban population and integrate intellectuals into the new political order" [Hunt 1992:465]. The involvement did appear to focus on the concern of the nation to restrain the group collectively identified as Chinese counter-revolutionaries. The old thesis, "Korea as lips to China's teeth," was still true.

Though a great deal of information has been accumulated concerning China's involvement, we are still at a loss to completely understand the essence of the relations between Stalin and Kim Il Sung. It is also true that we know far less than we would like about the position of the Chinese Communist Party, apart from–perhaps even in opposition to–the often arbitrary rule of Mao.

The best statement about China's role might well be Allan Whiting's: "Neither Moscow-dominated nor irrational, the Chinese leadership . . . acted essentially out of fear of a 'determined, powerful enemy on China's doorstep'" [as quoted in Hunt 1992:465-470].

THE REPUBLIC OF (SOUTH) KOREA

The Communists' histories of the war in Korea claim that the war began with an act of aggression by the forces of Syngman Rhee. The North Korean government has claimed to have secret documents to prove that South Korean plans for an invasion began as early as 1949. President Rhee, this view suggests, thought this was necessary to avoid the collapse of his government. This point of view suggests that President Rhee was acting on the orders of Gen. Omar Bradley, U. S. Army Chief of Staff. If South Korea did not attack first, the theory continues, it at least planned and initiated the attack. America's desire in this was to expand its influence in Asia and to prevent the overthrow Syngman Rhee.

Others suggest that the South Korean leader provoked war in an effort to consolidate his divided nation and gain U.S. support for unification. The provocations took many forms, but some claim–I. F. Stone and Karunakar Gupta in particular–that Rhee may well have sent troops across the border and into North Korea [Gupta 1972:699-716]. In fact, there is a claim, not yet well sorted out, that during these early attacks the South Korean forces captured the village of Haeju on the North Korean side of the 38th Parallel, just above the Ongjin Peninsula. The belief is that once North Korea responded, Rhee directed his troops to retreat in order to force the United States to commit troops to prevent the fall of his government.

Syngman Rhee, who had been president of the Korean provisional government since 1919, was openly critical of the policy to divide Korea and of the U.S. acceptance of the division. Powerful rather than popular, Syngman Rhee was elected president of the new Republic of Korea. Following the elections in August 1945, in which he was supported by the United Nations, Rhee reaffirmed that his goal was the unification of Korea. Rhee saw the development of the Democratic People's Party of Korea as a threat. In his mind, the war of unification had been going on, militarily and politically, for years.

Thus it seems wise to take seriously the idea, supported by Joyce and Gabriel Kolko among others [Kolko 1972], that the Korean War was but one phase of a long struggle between Korean nationalists of whatever persuasion. It was not, as Americans have liked to believe, a radical change from peace to war.

While these explanations may seem extreme, there is little doubt that South Korea had been provoking North Korea for some time, or that President Rhee, while wishing to avoid defeat, was not totally unhappy with the outbreak of war. He was very pleased to have the United States involved in his dream.

Commenting later on the American decision to engage, President Rhee reported, "U.S. intervention in Korea was the greatest and noblest act of recent American history," saving South Korea from "totalitarian conquest and buying time for the west to rearm"[MacArthur 1963:62].

THE UNITED STATES

The official American view was that the attack had taken America completely by surprise. This is most likely true. When it happened it was seen as the prelude to Soviet military action in Europe. President Truman was convinced that his only real options were a commitment now to this localized war in Korea or involvement later in a total war with Russia. There were many who felt that any expanded war would necessarily be nuclear, and many believed that the outbreak in Korea was the beginning of World War III. When the anticipated attack in Europe failed to occur, the defenders of this view adopted the "attrition theory," claiming that the invasion of Korea was designed to weaken the American ability to respond elsewhere.

President Truman's first reaction, expressed at the summer White House in Independence, Missouri, was typical of the man. Even following this outburst, his decision to fight came as a surprise to both the Communist world and the American leadership. "We are going to fight," he told his daughter Margaret, to an aide he said, "We can't let the U. N. down." This "wretched little satellite government as [as Truman referred to North Korea] cannot be allowed to get away with this." To another he commented, "By God, I'm going to let them have it" [Blair 1987:67].

It seems odd that the United States was so surprised. The surprise is often blamed on President Rhee's deliberate silence about the extensive build-up of North Korean troops, or on the failure of the fledgling CIA to understand what was happening in North Korea. It is even claimed General MacArthur's intelligence efforts were not very productive. But, not everyone was surprised. The editors of *Saturday Evening Post*, in an editorial as early as September 1950, informed their readers that they had seen the war coming–and in anticipation had dispatched war correspondents to the cover the fighting when it broke out. Others suggest that the United States had taken several precautions prior to the North Korean invasion, including the drafting of a resolution for the United Nations Security Council.

The cause of American involvement lies deep within its revolutionary spirit, as well as in the need for a practical response to the dictates of the Cold War. America was, at least psychologically, supportive of the Korean desire for freedom from foreign domination and, to a lesser degree, for the unification of its culture. But there was little real interest in Korea for itself.

In 1947, Lt. Gen. John Hodge determined that it would take forty-five thousand men to occupy Korea. The then secretary of war, Robert P. Patterson, thought the cost would be too great; the secretary recommended to Forrestal that the army pull out of South Korea. The occupation continued, but the Joint

Chiefs of Staff expressed the view that there was little strategic value in continuing the continued presence of troops and bases in Korea. Even in the extreme case that the United States might enter Asia militarily, the plan would be to avoid the Korean Peninsula.

The decision to go into Korea had a great deal to do with the American understanding of international communism, as well as with President Truman's limited grasp of grand strategy. Truman, unlike Franklin D. Roosevelt, was not interested in making his own foreign policy; he preferred to hear the arguments and sign-off on the decision. He was not strong in this area. Also, he failed to support his strong stand on the containment of communism with an equally strong army. In failing to do so, he invited challenges.

The poor condition of the military was, of course, not totally Truman's fault. Major blame can be placed on the conservative Republicans in Congress. They were still seeped in prewar isolation and unwilling to grant the funds needed for security. These men and women assumed that the great threat to America was at home. Besides, if came to war, Korea had the great advantage of being a proxy war. It was a war to be fought on the land of another people. It is also true that Truman was frightened of Stalin. At least, he was afraid of Stalin's irrationality. Interestingly, newly available Soviet documents have made it very clear that Joseph Stalin was equally afraid of provoking the United States into war. Trying to avoid such a war, President Truman seemed aware that if he had to react to Soviet probes, Korea was one of the few places where he might do so without running too great a risk.

Clay Blair, an insightful historian of this period suggests that the president was greatly influenced by a "battery captain's attitude"–an attitude reflected in his assumption that the military were always "flimflamming" for more funds. Cutting military spending was ill advised, as was the unbridled talk of members of his administration. Robert T. Oliver, in his *Why We Came to Korea,* in 1950 suggests that the war was the result of a series of blunders and misunderstanding as well as America's unwillingness to stand up to the Russians [Oliver 1950]. C. Clyde Mitchell, in *Korea: Second Failure in Asia,* suggested in 1951 that that the United States entry was not the cause of the war but a legitimate reaction [Mitchell 1951]. American involvement demonstrated to the world that the Russian advance could be stopped [Kaufman 1981:1]. Dean Acheson believed that only by a dramatic commitment could the Americans convince the Soviet Union it would not be pushed around.

Some would argue that Truman's positive response in the Korean War effectively rebuffed the expansionist tendencies of the Soviet Union. In fact, after the success at Inchon, the Truman administration held secret discussions about the direction of the war, in which there emerged an obvious interest in "showing" Moscow, by the armed liberation of one of its satellites. It may well be true that the Korean War demonstrated to the Soviet Union that the United

States would respond, with armed force if necessary, to any aggression on the part of the Communists. But the United States government was also aware that it was not necessarily a wise move to push it [Kemp 1989].

George Kennan of the Department of State and CIA director, Paul Nitze, were concerned about the push into North Korea and voiced opposition. They were afraid that Stalin would consider it an act of aggression against the "communist movement"and would become involved. They suggested he might even encourage the Chinese to enter the war. Stephen Pelz affirmed that "Truman and Acheson needed to interpret the North Korean attack as part of a global challenge to justify reversing their Asian policy" [Cumings 1997:31]. Burton I. Kaufman, who examined the events of 1945-50, suggests that the war was most likely a great power struggle between the United States and the Soviet Union. It was the pressure of this power struggle, between the two emerging superpowers that allowed the primarily civil conflict between the North and the South to expand into an international war [Kaufman 1986]

Dean Acheson has been given a short shift by historians, and it is probably true in fact he did not understood the emerging China as well as he thought he did. It can be argued that he miscalculated the determination of China's new communist government. Sen. Kenneth Wheir of Nebraska charged that "the blood of our boys in Korea was on Acheson's shoulders." The China lobby in Congress proclaimed that Acheson had lost China, because he did not provide massive aid to Chiang Kai-shek. In turn, Chiang despised the American effort to settle the differences between Nationalist China and Mao. Japan played a key role as well in America's position, for there was never any doubt that Japan was politically important and would play an increasingly important role in the future. This prospect pitted Japan's economic future against the Pentagon's "global strategic vision" until the outbreak of the war changed things [Foot 1991:425].

Some consideration must be given to the fact the Truman administration was not as solid as it is often remembered. Truman made some important decisions, but he also must be held accountable for some less than decisive actions. Acheson at first urged Truman to get congressional approval before entering the war, but Truman chose to exercise presidential prerogative. His unwillingness, or perhaps inability much earlier, to deal with MacArthur greatly aggravated the situation. At least, it must be recognized that Mao's understanding of the relationship between military and political action was, if not better than Truman's, at least more decisive. It is also good to keep in mind that this was a period of intense anticommunism. Later in the war the Cincinnati major league baseball team would under pressure change its name for a short time from "Reds" to "Redlegs" [Kerin 1994:365].

There has been some excellent work done on the causes of the war, and there appears to be enough responsibility to go around. Several theories of blame have emerged, ranging from outright Soviet aggression to complex patterns of regional tension, and international versus national communism.

Certainly the work of Bruce Cumings, John Merrill, Rosemary Foot, and others has advanced the study a long way. Kathryn Weathersby's "Soviet Aims in Korea and the Origins of the Korean War, 1945-50: New Evidence from Russian Archives" [145] and Xi Zhang's "China's entry into the Korean War" [Xi 1993:1-30] have both provided translations of Soviet and Chinese works that introduce new answers and, with them, new questions.

Chapter 5

Some of the Controversies

"We're still attacking and we're going all the way to the Yalu.
Don't let a bunch of Chinese laundrymen stop you."

Gen. Charles A. Willoughby

Histories of the Korean War often move through the narrative with such generalizations that they miss as much as they reveal. In most cases this is due to the lack of substantial monographs and in-depth studies upon which to draw for the less-known facts and consideration of the controversial areas. The political factors that directed events often made the actions that is taken seem unreasonable. Often unidentified expectations and poorly defined agendas contribute to the difficulty in understanding. Because is it was not always clear what we wanted then, there is often a controversy now about what happened.

Thus many issues remain unmentioned or are simply dropped on readers with little information or analysis. Likewise, there are many issues about which there continues to be disagreement. This American war was fought without congressional authority and stopped without victory. It began unexpectedly and ended in a cease-fire. The end solved few of the original concerns. The following are some questions often asked; they are representative of the issues still being argued.

WAS THE KOREAN WAR LEGAL?

Probably not! It was not identified as a war until late in the 1950s, when Congress so designated it. In the most obvious use of the term, it was not legal: that is, it was not constitutional. Authority for U.S. entry into the Korean War amounted to a quick decision, based on an appeal to tradition. It was an important moment in history: President Truman's decision established a prerogative that has been used by American presidents ever since. Truman felt he had every right to send troops to fight–if not by the authority given him as commander-in-chief, then perhaps on the authority of the United Nations. But the charter of the United Nations does not, nor did it then, supersede the

Constitution of the United States.

President Truman was to argue that history was on his side. At the president's request the State Department constructed a list of prior incidents where a president committed American troops without congressional action. The list was impressive. In many cases, however, it was misleading, and in others totally irrelevant. Most were situations in which the president exercised his authority to defend American lives or property, or to provide security for Americans during periods of civil strife. Most did not, as was the case in Korea, interfere with the actions of a sovereign state. It takes Congress to declare war, but that is required to send armed forces to acts as guards, policeman, or peacemakers is a presidential decree. President Truman described his decision to send troops to Korea as a "police action." At no point did he asked for the authority to act. The conflict in Korea was the President's War.

There had been some talk of seeking congressional consideration, but Acheson managed to stop it. Having reconsidered his earlier opinion, he was afraid if given the chance, members of Congress would use the opportunity to argue against the war. Even if the legislators finally passed a war resolution, the debate would give the Soviets some reason to believe America was not totally committed. In the end Truman, had to be pressured into telling Congress.

Truman's response to the outbreak of war was a pragmatic one, and even if illegal, it appears to have been popular. George Gallup calculated that 80 percent of the American people supported President Truman's decision [Rose 1999:192]. Looking back, it appears that decisive action was indeed required, and there was hardly time for him to take the traditional route. Should Truman have asked Congress for a declaration of war? That may be a political and ethical question as much as a legal one, but many believe that if Truman had not acted quickly, intervention would have come too late.

Another, related question should be addressed as well. What if Congress *had* been asked to declare war on North Korea? Would the American people have maintained their support longer? If the war had been properly declared, would its popularity have continued even after things began to go wrong? Of course, how would the nature of the Cold War have changed if at this point both the United States and the Soviet Union allowed it to heat up ?

Behind this question of legality, however, is a larger issue. How war is waged depends fundamentally upon what war is conceived to be. Many did not understand what this one was about nor why it was necessary for the United States to commit itself once again to a foreign conflict. Historically, the pronouncement of a war–the declaration–has defined images that are then carried into the war–that is, the goal and thus the applicable rules. The lack of declaration meant that the rules of behavior were unclear.

WHY DID THE RUSSIAN DELEGATE MISS THE "WAR RESOLUTION" IN THE UNITED NATIONS?

Many histories of the Cold War and the Korean War feel the United States was lucky to have won United Nations support for the resolution declaring North Korea as the aggressor nation. The approval was possible because the Soviet ambassador, who could have vetoed it, was not in attendance at the Security Council meeting where the resolution was passed. He had walked out during an earlier debate over the admission of Communist China as a member.

Two important things have come to light since the opening of the Soviet archives. One is that the Soviet Union was not all that happy about Red China being admitted to the United Nations. Such an admission would make it too easy for Communist China to establish powerful ties with the West. Having the ambassador walk out during the discussion allowed the Soviet government to avoid a lose-lose situation. The Soviet Union wanted to vote neither for, nor against, Red China's admission. Later, when the question of Korea came up, and the American resolution came before the assembly, the ambassador was told not to return.

The reason as it is understood, was basic: if Russia vetoed the resolution, Stalin was afraid that the United States would enter the conflict on its own. There was a pact between the Soviet Union and North Korea concerning the defense of Korea if the United States attacked. If the United States decided to go it alone, Stalin would have been obligated to the possibility of a face to face confrontation. If, however, the American resolution passed, it would be the United Nations that was in conflict with North Korea. The Soviets had no commitment with North Korea concerning that contingency. It is too simplistic to suggest that Russian used America, or the United Nations, to get what it wanted. The records do not support such a case. But it must be understood that Stalin was able to put the best face on a situation full of danger.

WAS THE UNITED NATIONS ACTION LEGAL?

The action was legal in terms of the United Nations Charter. Certainly the United Nations had every right to condemn the North Korean aggression and to ask its member nations to come to the aid of the Republic of Korea. A more significant question might be, however, the degree to which the United Nations acted free without American pressure. There are many who believe that the United Nations was actually a puppet for the American agenda, the American involvement, protected by a United Nations resolution, was a facade designed to defend the ever expanding interests in Japan. This probably is not true, even though there is no doubt that the United States had a great deal of influence on the international body.

The member nations had their own needs, and they voted in a manner that served their best interests. Yet to a degree they were pressured. Most certainly the military aspect of the United Nations involvement was under American control, especially after Gen. Douglas MacArthur was named supreme commander of United Nations Forces.

One way to consider the degree of American influence is to consider the contributions of the other nations, looking first at the ground forces. At the peak the United Nations had under 950,000 troops on the ground. Of these the United States and the Republic of Korea accounted for less than 890,000. An additional thirty-nine thousand or so troops were available from the commonwealth nations. The remaining twenty-four thousand plus hardly represented a major military commitment. On the other hand United Nations member nations provided naval and air units, hospital ships and medical units, supplies, and most important, the commitment of the Western world against communism. Later, this method–a coalition of free nations–would be used to great advantage by Presidents George Bush and Bill Clinton.

DID SECRETARY OF STATE DEAN ACHESON'S "UNCONCERNED ABOUT KOREA" SPEECH CLEAR THE WAY FOR THE NORTH KOREAN INVASION OF SOUTH KOREA?

Dean Acheson made a speech to the National Press Club on January 12, 1950 in which he clearly placed Korea outside the policy concerns of the United States. The purpose of his speech, apparently, was to rebut Republican charges that the Democrats were "soft" on the Communists. This charge had come up quite often after the Communist takeover of mainland China. Acheson suggested that South Korea was growing ever stronger, and that the new government had an excellent chance of avoiding communism on its own. He accordingly, affirmed that the American defensive perimeter excluded Korea.

In hindsight it looks like a very unwise speech. But at the time the secretary of state was acting out of the belief that the defense of Korea was a United Nations problem. He certainly was articulating American policy, such as it was. Taking the speech at face value, Acheson's comments reflected the attitude of the Truman administration. This was an attitude that can only be interpreted as having little interest in what happened in Korea.

Critics, understandably, suggest that Acheson's speech provided North Korea an open invitation to attack. Some speculate that Kim Il Sung, having heard the speech, felt that he had permission to act. There is evidence that both the Soviet Union and North Korea took note of the speech. Certainly, the idea that the United States was not interested enough to interfere would have made the prospect of war far more acceptable.

The underlying assumption of the speech was that the United States would fight communism by means of economic aid and by providing support for democratic governments. Despite the loss of China to communism, the implication was that other nations could be saved by American support of economic strength and stable government. Such stability, could it be achieved, was the primary threat to communism everywhere.

WHY DID THE UNITED NATIONS MOVE ITS TROOPS ACROSS THE 38TH PARALLEL AFTER HAVING ACHIEVED THE MISSION OUTLINED BY THE UN RESOLUTION?

The United Nations called upon its members for aid in the expulsion of the military forces of the Democratic People's Republic of Korea from the soil of its southern neighbor. Twenty-seven nations responded. By mid-September 1950, the goal of freeing South Korea from foreign occupation had been accomplished. Why then did the United Nations cross the 38th Parallel into North Korea?

The decision was to set off a new, or at least different, war. Most members of the Truman administration shared MacArthur's opinion that the United Nations forces should pursue the North Korean army while they had it on the run. The time to destroy the enemy was when it was weak and retreating. Besides, it was necessary to cross the 38th Parallel and defeat the forces of North Korean to provide South Korea with protection from new aggression. General MacArthur believed the only way to prevent North Korea from launching another attack was to occupy North Korean territory. Besides, total victory would allow the peninsula to be united once again under the banner of the United Nations.

Truman apparently made the decision. On September 27, 1950, the president authorized MacArthur to operate north of the 38th Parallel. The General Assembly of the United Nations legitimized this decision on October 7, 1950. But this was a change in the goals, and some of the member nations were less than supportive. Increasing disagreement among member nations was to inject confusion. Truman's decision to cross the 38th Parallel caused mixed feelings among those involved. Some of America's allies felt that if the United Nations did not occupy North Korea the Russians might try to occupy it. Some believed that even if the territory of North Korea were occupied and troops moved toward the Yalu, there would be no danger of Russian involvement. China was another question.

President Rhee was certainly not anxious to stop. He wanted to unite Korea by any means. The Truman administration was in full agreement about the unification of Korea under a government opposed to communism. The military opposed the Department of Defense, and the Department of State was hotly divided within itself. The United Nations seemed willing to make whatever concession the United States wanted. It appears that the Joint Chiefs of Staff were unwilling to take a strong stand against anything MacArthur requested; they were still in awe of the success of the Inchon landing. They now went along with his agenda without full consideration of its implications. In any case, at least in the minds of some of the United Nations members, Korea was a single nation, and thus the 38th Parallel was artificial.

Once the United Nations crossed the 38th Parallel MacArthur pushed for the elimination of the armies of North Korea. As a military goal it was fairly straightforward, but the methods needed to accomplish it were not nearly as obvious. The announced goal of unifying Korea was seen by the Chinese as a threat to their security. But it was also introduced a political corollary that might be very difficult for the UN to accomplish short of total victory.

Looking back on it, there is little doubt that China's entry into the war could have been averted and the war concluded in the autumn of 1950, if the United States had been more restrained. But therein lies the heart of yet another controversy. General MacArthur's behavior suggested he would welcome a war with China, or at least did not fear it. The United Nations commander did not take seriously the warnings of the Chinese premier, Chou-En Lai, that China would become involved. MacArthur's intelligence officers continued to affirm that the Chinese would not enter the war in any significant number. In mid-October the trap was sprung.

The decision to advance the war into North Korea resulted in part from the five assumptions held by the U.S. Joint Chiefs that in September 1950 were still in vogue: future wars would be precipitated by the Soviet Union; the war, when it came, would be total; successful deterrence or ultimate victory would be achieved by air strikes; the Soviet Union would not risk being involved in a major war until it had a stockpile of atomic weapons; it was far easier, and cheaper, to place total reliance on one branch of the service than to maintain a balanced force.

The decision, however did little for Truman's credibility among his domestic and international audience. One historian suggests "America's decision to defend South Korea was unexpected and daring. The decision to cross the 38th and drive toward the Yalu seriously challenged American foreign policy and eventually brought down the Truman administration" [Blair 1987:28].

WAS THE UNITED STATES READY FOR WAR?

No, it certainly was not. At the end of World War II, the size and complexity of the military were drastically cut. The navy scrapped or mothballed a good portion of its fleet, the marines were reduced to little more than ship and embassy guards, and reservists and many National Guard troops were released. Only the U. S. Air Force, newly designated, and carrying the totally unrealistic burden of being the defender of the nation, was experiencing any growth at all. Besides, the services were fighting among themselves as Congress continued to cut their budgets.

By the time of the North Korean invasion, President Truman, and his secretary of defense, Louis Johnson, had wrought considerable havoc within the conventional forces of the United States. The president and the military were at odds over the proper balance of a military force. Truman apparently did not see the connection between the strong stand he was making on the containment of communism and the necessity of a strong military. Responding to criticism of a proposed defense budget, the president admitted he was cutting the services' budgets but he refused to admit there was any reason for concern about military preparedness.

Within three years of the end of World War II, the U.S. Army had lost most of its cutting edge. Troops available were not well trained. In order to save money, basic training had been cut to eight weeks. Later, basic was advanced to fourteen weeks, but that included speciality training. Those who enlisted in the postwar army were a different breed from their wartime predecessors. This was, as well, a different kind of enlistment. Most of those who entered the service at this time were interested in adventure, but of the peaceful type; they thought in terms more of occupation duty than of war.

When President Truman committed the nation, he and his advisors put considerable pressure on the military. The troops available for immediate deployment were "occupation troops," with all that implies in terms of poor and limited training, inexperience, and incomplete equipment. Besides, even the units that were available were short of personnel. Instead of the three battalions normally assigned in an infantry regiment, there were two. The same was also true of the artillery units.

The leadership was not much better. Two excellent scholars, D. Clayton James and Ronald H. Spector, have looked into the World War II record of Gen. Douglas MacArthur and concluded that his actions were impulsive. It would it would appear, he was impulsive again when he recommended the commitment of American ground forces in South Korea. If his acts were not impulsive, then they were poorly conceived. In the first place intervention broke a long military tradition, based on sound policy, of not committing troops to fight Asians on the Asian mainland. But perhaps more egregious, and more directly MacArthur's responsibility, was counting on the Eighth U.S. Army, which was grossly under strength, unprepared, and demoralized.

General MacArthur, like his intelligence officers, greatly underestimated the North Korean's intentions. When it came time to send his ill-prepared troops to fight in South Korea, the impact of the budget cuts became very apparent. To begin with it was decided to send an advanced unit of the 24th Infantry Division to South Korea, the U. S. Navy had to scrounge transportation from other sources to move it. This unit, known as Task Force Smith after its commander, Lt. Col. Charles B. "Brad" Smith, was the first to fight. He was committed on July 5. Despite a courageous stand, Task Force Smith suffered a disastrous defeat at Osan, by the Fourth Infantry Division of the North Korean People's Army, backed by T-34 tanks of the 209th Armored Brigade. Smith's outfit bought time that the United Nations desperately needed. It also upset the timetable established by Kim Il Sung. At this period, every moment counted. The whole division would pay a price in those early months. The 24th Infantry Division ultimately took sixteen thousand men into the fight. When it was relieved by the forward units of the First Cavalry Division on July 22, 1950, the division had been reduced to 8,660.

The tank available to United Nations troops at this time was the M-24 Chaffee light reconnaissance tank , with a 75 mm gun. It was no match for the Soviet-built T-34, which carried an 85 mm gun. Neither were America's 2.36 inch antitank guns of much value against the Soviet tanks supporting of the North Korean troops. Newer and more effective antitank guns were not yet in the country. Radios, many of which had been in storage since the end of World

War II, did not work. To make it all worse, the ammunition supplied was not what was needed.

WHY DID GENERAL DOUGLAS MAC ARTHUR DIVIDE HIS FORCES BETWEEN EIGHTH ARMY AND X CORPS WHEN MOVING TOWARD THE YALU RIVER?

Preparing for the landing at Inchon, MacArthur reconstituted X Corps and placed it under a separate command. He intended that Eighth Army, under Lt. Gen. Walton H. "Johnny" Walker, would remain engaged in the protective perimeter around Pusan. To command the new corps he selected his chief of staff, Maj. Gen. Edward M. Almond. It was formed by combining the First Marine Division and Seventh Infantry Division (Army). After the successful Inchon landing, Eighth Army broke out from Pusan, the two commands came together for the taking of Seoul.

When Seoul had been returned to President Rhee, General MacArthur decided to maintain the separation of his two commands. He moved them to the east coast–the First Marine Division by sea, and the Seventh Infantry Division by rail and sea. The two commands landed at Wonsan and Iwon respectively. His intention was to move them westward as the eastern pincer, against Pyongyang; Eighth Army was the western pincer. When the North Korean capital fell, MacArthur reoriented X Corps, moving it north to the Yalu. Eighth Army headed north on the west side of the mountain. He coordinated the two commands from his headquarters in Tokyo.

As X Corps–now including the U.S. Third Infantry Division–and Eighth Army moved into North Korean territory, the separation between them became increasingly dangerous. At times the gap was as much as eighty miles, a distance aggravated by the terrain, which made radio communications between the two commands difficult.

General MacArthur, as would many of his apologists, indicated that X Corps was not an offensive but a tactical probe–the drive toward the Yalu was in a "reconnaissance in force,"to determine the intentions of the Chinese forces. General MacArthur would argue that his effort forced Red China to abandon its plan, and reveal the presence of the waiting troops. The fact that it did so does not, of course, justify the action; nor does it prove that a reconnaissance was what the general had in mind. Maj. Gen. Charles Willoughby and Maj. Gen. Courtney Whitney provide us the same basic story, using the same words, seeming to suggest common authorship.[Stueck 1995:401]

While the Pyongyong offensive was in progress, MacArthur's headquarters concluded that both Eighth Army on the west, and X Corps ,on the east, were in good enough logistical shape to renew the attack to the north. General Almond apparently had no difficulty with the physical nature of the command separation, but General Walker was less at ease. Walker made some preparations for the withdrawal he felt might come, and he deliberately stalled his offensive. In doing so he had to deal with MacArthur's impatience and with questions about supplies and lines of communication.

Maj. Gen. Oliver P. Smith, commander of the First Marine Division, was upset about MacArthur's assessment of the situation and with MacArthur's continued role even after the intervention of Chinese troops. It soon became evident, at least to the field commanders, that the two United Nations forces were no longer competing to see which could penetrate the deeper. They both were having serious doubt about their abilities to maintain and supply themselves.

In light of the unorthodox separation of forces and the eventual defeat of X Corps at the hands of the Chinese advance, hardly looked like just a reconnaissance in force. To many it seemed MacArthur was attempting to cover a mistake. Later, MacArthur supporters would suggest that the Joint Chiefs of Staff knew of MacArthur's plan to separate his commands and advance to the Yalu, and approved of it. The inference was that the Joint Chiefs agreed that MacArthur's advance was more a reconnaissance than not. No evidence has yet appeared in the records of the Joint Chiefs to support this thesis. Lieutenant General Collins, speaking at the congressional hearings, explained that all the Joint Chiefs could do was accept General MacArthur's view.

The fact remains that General MacArthur ordered the commitment of his troops with such slim reserves that in any ensuing conflict the enemy would have the initiative. Even General Willoughby, who defended MacArthur on every possible occasion, admitted that the UN command "was gambling" when it launched its offensive into the "hornets' nest" [DeWeerd 1962:435-452].

The question remains, why did MacArthur advance? Many historians blame it on MacArthur's arrogance, his egotistical belief in his own ability to predetermine the behavior of the enemy. It is hard to disagree with this. We know that he was not happy with General Walker's lack of aggressiveness, and that he placed a great deal of faith in General Almond. He apparently was not concerned that the Korean landscape cut off one coast from the other. Nor did he respond to the fact that the farther he allowed his forces to move toward the Yalu River, the more difficult communications and logistics became.

WHY WAS MAC ARTHUR SO SURPRISED BY THE CHINESE ATTACK IN NOVEMBER 1950?

It may be too harsh to suggest that the Supreme Commander was surprised. It is hard to believe that MacArthur did not know there were Chinese troops gathered at the Yalu and that a significant number had crossed over into Korea. What he apparently failed to understand was their intention and the size of their force.

Through the generally neutral nation of India, the United States tried to tell China, on the day after Inchon, that the United Nations meant no threat to China's independence. The Chinese leader was unimpressed. Mao Tse-tung believed America "deliberately concocted the assault of the Syngman Rhee gang against the Korean Democratic People's Republic of Korea in order to expand its aggression in the East" [Rose 1999:230]

There are many accounts of the Chinese decision to become involved. Emerging records now allow a serious analysis of Beijing's response to the crisis in Korea. Certainly China's interests in the affairs of North Korea were more than a simple concern of a neighbor. Mao was troubled about the U.S. promise to protect Formosa. One result of a North Korean invasion would be to tie America to a war on the Asian mainland, eating up its resources, and –it was hoped–making it more difficult for them to continue to commit to Formosa. Emerging records now allow a serious analysis of Beijing's response to the crisis in Korea. Regardless of the specific reason, however, the Chinese entry provided a near-classic example of "strategic surprise."

It is difficult to see the American response to the situation as anything other than a mishandling of intelligence. There had been several warnings. Not the least was a Chinese government effort to warn the United States through the Indian ambassador. America's ally Great Britain also warned the United States that if it sent Americans across the 38th Parallel, the Communist Chinese would enter the war. MacArthur chose to ignore the implications of these warnings.

In in the field, the evidence of Chinese involvement was strong, and Walker, and Smith, were concerned. This was true as well of several other commanders at various levels, who were very much aware that they were fighting Chinese troops. As early as October 1950, Chinese soldiers began to appear among the prisoners of war captured in a series of skirmishes. General Peng The-huai, in command of the troops that hit the American line, was discouraged about the effect of their brief attack. "All we seem to have accomplished is to convince the Americans that Chinese troops have not entered Korean in any strength." [Pearlman 1999:304].

Part of the American mistake was the failure to realize that the average Chinese soldier was far better informed than an American enlisted man would be about the activities of his army. The individual soldier among Chinese volunteers was aware of the size of the Chinese buildup and knowledgeable about the intended goals of the campaign. When American intelligence agents asked the Chinese prisoners about out the character of the attack, the prisoners freely told them In a good many cases they simply were not believed. What was difficult to accept, apparently, was not that the Chinese troops were gathering along the Yalu but that a Chinese private would have valid information concerning the proposed attack.

General MacArthur had promised President Truman, at their Wake Island meeting in October 1950, that the Chinese would not intervene. He had been bold enough to promise President Truman that if by chance China should enter the fight, the presence of Chinese troops would present no problem to the UN command. He must have misunderstood the size and intensity of the Chinese military endeavor, and most likely he underestimated the determination of the Chinese Communists. The U.S. intelligence community may have had such information, as it has often claimed, it was not able to convince the military.

Thus, the United Nations was at a disadvantage concerning the intentions of the enemy; field plans were being made on the basis on bad information. On the other hand, the Chinese People's Volunteers could learn much of what they needed about United Nations plans by simply listening to the broadcasts of American journalists.

Major General Willoughby, MacArthur's intelligence officer, continually denied that the Chinese were involved. Willoughby, who liked to call MacArthur a classic warrior, was unqualified for his job, in many respects, MacArthur was his own intelligence officer. The brutal fact is that neither he nor any other responsible officers anticipated the early attack. Nor, once it happened, were they able to understand properly the lull that occurred in late October and early November of 1950. It was a period of miscalculation.

Bin Yu suggests that the Chinese attacked originally to test how its troops would fare against ROK forces, and that the Chinese pulled back and disappeared as part of a plan to trap United Nations troops. The Chinese certainly made every effort to create the perception of a disorderly retreat. The message they were trying to convey was that they had been forced to stop the engagement because they were so short of supplies. Part of the Chinese plan was the release of more than one hundred prisoners - of - war. Twenty -seven of the prisoners released in this effort to confuse the United Nations were Americans. The Chinese had told the prisoners that they were being released because supply difficulties were forcing the Chinese People's Volunteers to return to China.

Even after the initial confrontation and breaking off, however, and despite reports from field officers and intelligence officers in the field, MacArthur continued to maintain the pretense that the Chinese prisoners who had been taken were nothing but individual soldiers fighting in North Korean commands. The action was, of course, a Maoist tactic learned in the long civil war: Lure the enemy deep, concentrated your forces under cover, attack suddenly while the enemy is moving, dispatch them with great speed.

WHY DID TRUMAN FIRE GENERAL MAC ARTHUR IN APRIL 1951?

President Truman fired Gen. Douglas MacArthur in April 1951, in what must be one of the most courageous decisions ever made by an American president. General MacArthur was well - known, well respected, and considered by many the savior of democracy. He had achieved a stature uncommon in American history. President Harry Truman, as commander-in-chief, fired his highest-ranking military commander for insubordination. The firing was not the immediate result, as had been suggested, of MacArthur's move north across the 38th Parallel; he had authorization for that. The general was fired because he failed to conform to the demands and instructions of his commander -in-chief. President Truman gave very few of the actual reasons when he addressed the American people on April 11, 1951. Many Americans simply did not understand what was going on.

Mail, in response to Truman's decision, ran 45 percent for and 55 percent against. Many agreed with the need to maintain the constitutional authority of the president. MacArthur, some suggested, was a symptom of the administration's failure to accept responsibility. On the negative side critics identified the total lack of foreign policy and international direction. Others, like historian Joseph Goulden, felt that MacArthur suffered from a major problem of ego, linked with sadism, and was blind to the realities of the war he was fighting.

Behind President Truman's decision, and a key to the seriousness of the events, was an effort to control the expansion of the war. Truman was determined not to let the war get out of hand. He was afraid that it could easily be expanded into World War III. He felt the wisest move would be to achieve some sort of cease-fire while protecting America's image at home and in the world.

A related issue, and an important one, for President Truman was the affirmation of constitutional civilian control over the military. President Truman, a vocal advocate of the power of the presidency, would not tolerate what he considered the failure of a military figure to recognize this basic civilian control. The fact that Truman had the support of the Joint Chiefs of Staff is a good indication that MacArthur's independence had become a problem, and that the Joint Chiefs desired to retake control of the military aspects of the war.

While civilian control is generally understood, there is more to it than the division of power between civilian and military individuals. One reason the balance is so difficult to maintain is the large number of the military, and military-minded people, in the civilian government. It is therefore very important that a field commander be in agreement with–or supportive of–the policies of the administration. To impose restrictions, especially of the Korean War variety, on the field commander requires a change in the traditional American attitude toward the military as instrument. If it is to work, the military must be in step with the administration, so that military operations are never conducted outside the accepted policy or attitude.

Perhaps the best illustration of the conflict between military practice and civilian expectation is found in the control of weapons. The weapons in this case were atomic. On one side the growing desperation of the military situation made use of the "big weapons" more and more advantageous. On the other side, if the United States were to use nuclear weapons in this confrontation, how many nations would want to be "saved" by this Western democracy? Admittedly, mutual restraint in this case probably helped to prevent the escalation of hostilities. The restraints were more difficult for those trained to believe, as did MacArthur , that "there is no substitute for victory."

The firing of General MacArthur enriched the alliance between the White House and the Joint Chiefs. It was an alliance built on the need for restraint in Korea, and the need to expand the military presence elsewhere. The next step was to name Maj. Gen. Matthew B. Ridgway to replace MacArthur in Japan. In Ridgway, President Truman was seeking someone who would control escalation and move as rapidly as possible toward peace. Later, Congress and the American people concluded President Truman had done the right thing.

WHAT HAPPENED TO GREAT BRITAIN'S PEACE PLAN?

The effort by the British government to achieve a peaceful settlement did not receive much support from the United States. At the time, the United States was not ready to come to a peace agreement. Perhaps more importantly, the United States was very reluctant to include a discussion of the "Chinese Question"–that is, the Nationalist Chinese on Formosa–as a part of any peace package.

The British Commonwealth nations, supported the American action in Korea. They were the first to send military forces. They had, however, balancing a very complex agenda. The agenda included keeping a good relationship with the United States; keeping America, and to some extent the United Nations, primarily focused on Europe; avoiding confrontations with Canada and India, both of whom had serious reservations about American intentions; and avoiding a shooting war with the Chinese.

Early in the war, as United Nations troops were pushing toward the Yalu, the British offered a plan designed to keep the war from expanding, called the "Buffer Zone Proposal." It would have created a demilitarized zone (DMZ) from Hungnam-Chonju to the Yalu River, a zone of protection for the Chinese border. Yet it would allow the United Nations to maintain some control over North Korean actions in the South. General MacArthur did not like it, and eventually the United States turned it down. So did the Chinese.

After President Truman's suggestion in a press conference that America might use atomic weapons, Great Britain became very concerned that America would allow the Korean confrontation to expand into a nuclear war. He sought to mediate between the United States and the USSR. He did so by proposing a compromise involving Korea and Formosa. The United States reluctantly supported the plan, at least in public, but there was considerable relief–not only in Washington, but also among the Nationalist Chinese–when the Chinese Communists rejected it.

The British government's concern over the possibilities of an expanded war, and its defense of China as a trading and economic partner led it into severe confrontations with the United States. While trouble was averted, the continued pressure by the British underscored differences both in world policy, and of commitment to the war itself.

IS THE "TWO WAR" THESIS A LEGITIMATE THEORY?

The two-war thesis has been a mainstay of Korean War historians for some time. There is much to support it. In this view, the North Korean phase, from the invasion on June 25, 1950, until the major Chinese push on November 25,

1950, is considered an American and United Nations victory. The "second war," the Chinese phase, from November 25, 1950, until the armistice in July 1953, was much less successful and is treated differently.

One way to look at these phases is to look at them in more philosophical terms, specifically "justified war" and "limited war." Phase one fits most of the criteria for what has historically been called limited war– the goals well set; the amount of force exerted equal to the task undertaken; and   expectations identified, so those involved can know when and if they are successful.

The Chinese phase might most easily be understood as a justified war, based on the criteria of "rightness." While our publicity asserted that the United States entered the war to save the Republic of Korea, and ultimately to achieve a much more abstract and international, goal, the containment of communism, the war with the Red Chinese was a war of survival and reprisal. It was a war against an enemy who had attacked us.

The two periods were not clearly separated from each other. They were contained in the same war. But there were differences in why and how they were fought.

WHY DID THE UNITED STATES NOT USE THE ATOMIC BOMB?

Given the contemporary efforts to avoid nuclear warfare, it is hard to imagine the possibility of the use of atomic bombs in the 1950s. But it was well within the range of possibility. President Truman had the advantage, and the disadvantage, of having ordered the use of atomic weapon twice before. While he certainly had no desire to use one again, his record made the possibility more realistic to both friends and enemies.

Several things affected the decision. A good portion of them were pragmatic; some, perhaps, were moral. One obvious reason was that the United States did not have very many such bombs. Another major limitation was that the weapons available in June 1950, were not designed for tactical use. Tactical nuclear weapons were still under development and would not be readily available until late 1951. Also, a primary question was how the weapons could be used to the United Nation's advantage.

A further consideration was that the Soviet Union possessed an atomic bomb, though how many Russian government had available was open to serious question. The possibility of a Soviet atomic response had to be acknowledged. Accordingly, however, consideration of the use of the bomb was related more to controlling the possible escalation of the war than to ending it. It is not surprising, then, that policy makers had frequent, and hotly debated, discussions over the potential role of nuclear weapons. Roger Dingman argues that the upshot was that the United States did not engage in coercive diplomacy but rather in a milder, non-nuclear, persuasive diplomacy [Dingman 1989:59-91].

One consideration for policy makers was that China did not take the nuclear threat as seriously as was necessary to make it completely useful as a deterrent. Some studies suggest the Chinese believed that the power of the bomb was greatly exaggerated. In the final analysis, they were prepared for any attack launched against them [Ryan 1989]. Accepted wisdom suggests that President Dwight D. Eisenhower's threat to use nuclear weapons made the Chinese return to the negotiation table in 1953 and forced them to stay long enough to arrive at a conclusion. President Eisenhower, after he left office, wrote in his memoirs:

One possibility was to let the Communist authorities understand, that, in the absence of satisfactory progress, we intended to move decisively without inhibition in our use of weapons, and would no longer be responsible for confining hostilities to the Korean Peninsula. We would not be limited by any worldwide gentleman's agreement. In India and in the Formosa Straits area, and at the truce negotiations at Panmunjom, we dropped the word, discreetly, of our intention. We felt quite sure it would reach Soviet and Chinese Communist ears [Eisenhower 1963:181].

In accepting that the United States waged a limited war–that is, a war designed to accomplish limited aims–it must also be acknowledged that the use of atomic weapons considered was proportional to that task. A nuclear strike against either China or North Korea would not, in terms of international reaction, have necessarily accomplished the stated objectives of the war.

In view of the complexity of the question, there may be some value in be learned from this generalization: the only weapons whose deployments have been successfully regulated in the history of warfare have been those of dubious military value, which belligerents were not inclined to use anyway. The atomic bomb may well fit into this generalization. Wars, even bloody ones like the Korean War, operate under rules. The rules are difficult to keep, but there are rules nevertheless. One of those rules is to *protect mutual self-interests.* That is, the military should not use tactics, or introduce weapons, that will create greater trouble and offer little military advantage.

WHY WERE THE COMMUNISTS ALLOWED AN AIR SANCTUARY IN MANCHURIA?

A great deal has been made of the "sanctuary" represented by the border of Manchuria. The long–held theory is that the U.S. planes, chasing North Korean and Chinese pilots through the skies of Korea, were forced to stop at the border and thus let them escape. The general assumption is that the United States wanted thereby to prevent the Chinese from using American border an excuse to expand the war. To some extent, this is true.

There were sanctuaries on both sides. In its own effort to avoid an escalation of the war, the Soviet Union warned the Chinese not to send their planes across the 38th Parallel. This was true as well of Soviet pilots, who, regularly flying missions against the United Nations, were prohibited from flying either over water–where they could be easily picked up if they were downed–or over the territory of South Korea in order to avoid capture. They were not to fly south of the Wonsan-Pyongyang line.

There is considerable evidence the Chinese sanctuary was violated. An American ace, Capt. Harold E. Fisher, was shot down over Dabao airfield, inside China, on April 7, 1953. The more evidence becomes available, the more obvious it becomes that U.S. planes flew regular missions designed to attack Chinese jets taking off from their home fields.

What was being aimed at by these "restrictions" is not well understood yet. But the reasons appear to have a great deal more to do with public acknowledgment of the attacks, than with the existence of them.

WHERE WAS THE CHINESE AIR FORCE?

The role of the Chinese air force has been underplayed, in light of the Soviet participation. Called the People's Liberation Army Air Force, it was created as a unit of the army just before the Korean War broke out. The Communist Chinese felt that an air arm was necessary if the nation's forces were successfully to attack the Nationalists' stronghold on Formosa. In some respects, the lack of interest in the Chinese air force arises from the low evaluations of North Korean and Chinese pilots, by United Nations pilots. It is understandable that American pilots preferred to believe they were fighting the more experienced and highly skilled Soviet pilots.

Nevertheless the Chinese air force played a highly significant role in the Korean War. Its effort was overshadowed by that of the Soviet air forces, but it was responsible for serious losses among United Nations–primarily American–aircraft over Korea.

WHY DID THE USSR AND THE UNITED STATES HIDE THE FACT THAT THEY WERE ENGAGED IN AIR BATTLES OVER KOREA?

The answer seems to be fairly simple. Neither side wanted to deal with the full implications of direct involvement. For decades little was said about the face-to- face confrontation. When asked, both nations categorically dissociated themselves from any such involvement.

Now, however, the evidence is beginning to appear as people involved are talking freely. Pilots of the Soviet air force stationed in China fought American pilots during the Korean War. The Soviet pilots fought over Korea using planes based in semi-security along the Manchurian border. The Soviets were required to wear Chinese uniforms and were trained to use Chinese phrases on the radio. In crisis, however, they reverted to their basic Russian. Some five thousand airmen were involved in the nearly two-year war. Lt. Gen. Georgi Lobov, commander of the 64th Fighter Air Corps in Korea, recalls that the Soviet pilots were very effective, especially against bombers and against fighters escorting the bombers. Their maneuverability restricted by the slower bombers made the fighters vulnerable to Soviet attack.

On the American side, there was real fear that if the American people knew there was direct confrontation between Soviet and American pilots, they would demand an escalation of the war. The Soviet authorities seemed to share the same fear. Stalin was not interested in going to war with the United States and he made considerable effort to avoid "proof" of his involvement. As for Truman, war resulted in a decline in his popularity. People were becoming discouraged with the conflict and dubbing it "Truman's War." He did not need the added problem of Soviet involvement.

The conflict was to the advantage of both sides. It was in the skies over North Korea that both nations tested their new air forces, tried out technological innovations, trained their pilots, and pushed planes to see what they could do. The air war in Korea played very much the same role as the Spanish Civil War, in the testing of modern weapons.

DID THE UNITED STATES ENGAGE IN BIOLOGICAL WARFARE?

In 1952 the Communists began claiming that the United States was using biological weapons. There was never any really hard evidence; the answers seem to depend on the meaning of the terms "chemical" and "biological." The question is, that if such tactics were used, why were they so ineffective? The United States had the tools, if it had decided on such a course of action. The American authorities denied the introduction of "germ warfare," but some inquirers suggested that they were less than honest.

There is no doubt that defoliants were used, that such bombs fell on civilians as well as soldiers, that people died of disease in those areas of bombardment, and that all of these might be identified as victims of some form of biological warfare. The charge was, in itself, a weapon. It hit the United States hard. The charges provided the Communist Chinese propaganda machine a valuable tool in the war against the "imperialists." Such charges became very effective in the "negotiations game."

Historian Kathryn Weathersby, of the Wilson Cold War International History Project at the Wilson Center in Washington, D.C., has been doing remarkable work with the newly opened Russian archives. Among other things she has uncovered evidence that the charges of "germ warfare" leveled against the United States in Korea were unfounded. Aided in her research by biochemist Milton Leitenbert, she has discovered that the Soviet, North Korean, and Chinese governments went to considerable effort in what amounted to gigantic, international "fraudulent theater."

Drawing from the reports of Lavrenti Beria, head of the Soviet Intelligence, at that time, she reports thousands were involved in this fake evidence and medical fraud. It was only after the death of Joseph Stalin, in 1953, that the Soviet Union no longer made these claims [Weathersby 1995].

American historians Jon Halliday and Bruce Cumings, as well as the well-respected British scientist Joseph Needham, have found evidence that supported the charges against the United States. The validity of this is evidence is compounded by the confessions of American airman who, as prisoners of war, made broadcasts concerning their "crimes," and by the strong American interest in the Japanese biological weapons program after the war.

We do know that chemical warfare was considered on one or two occasions. General Ridgway, facing the possibility of being pushed into the Sea of Japan, requested permission to use poison gas against the Chinese if, at the last minute, he could not hold. General MacArthur refused [Soffer 1998:118].

We can be sure that we have not heard the end of this argument. A new book has recently appeared, *The United States and Biological Warfare: Secrets from the Early Cold War and Korean War*, by Stephen Endicott and Edward Hagerman [1998]. It discusses American use of chemical and biological weapons during the Korean War. This new evidence makes it increasingly difficult to accept Secretary of State Dean Acheson's original denial of American involvement in such a program.

WHY DID RHEE FINALLY "GIVE IN" ON THE CEASE-FIRE?

President Rhee was so unpopular, both at home and among the serving American troops, that it was nearly impossible to establish a mandate for his protection or salvation. Quite honestly, Rhee's particular view was of little significance to the United Nations, or even to the United States.

Syngman Rhee was not in favor of the armistice, and in face, he never signed it. He wanted to unite North and South Korea. He was so angered by the possibility of a cease-fire that he released thousands of prisoners of war, in an effort to upset the negotiations. But the United States was determined, and it eventually bought off Rhee with a mutual - defense guarantee.

As far as the United States was concerned, the primary question was whether it should assume responsibility for protecting the world from communist aggression. If so, how could it determine which areas needed to be protected, and which areas could defend themselves?

South Korea was designated as one of those places in which American money and arms were necessary to secure the status quo. Once that was decided, Rhee could be brought along with promises of aid and protection. Just in case, other possibilities were considered by the military. (For a discussion of this, see "Operation Everready.")

WHERE WAS THE NAVY?

The U.S. Navy was involved in the Korean War from the beginning. It has never received the recognition due. It is at least partially because of the violent character of the ground war. One of President Truman's first decisions was to send the Seventh Fleet to guard the Formosa Strait. He called upon the navy to protect dependents being evacuated and for ammunition be transported from Japanese stockpiles. Before long, the navy was involved in interdiction, fire support, blockade, and siege.

The American fleet, supported by ships of member nations, was an active and critical participant from the opening shot. A carrier task force, Task Force 77, provided close air support for ground troops, interdiction, and bombardment. Patrol squadrons provided reconnaissance. Hastily assembled minesweepers cleared the sea-lanes under the fire of North Korean shore batteries.

An amphibious force was responsible for the landings at Inchon and Wonsan, as well as numerous other smaller actions. The fleet supported the perimeter at Pusan, established and maintained the long lines of supply throughout the war. Blockade ships controlled naval actives along both coasts, and on several significant occasions they evacuated United Nations forces. There were, in addition, attacks on Communist supply centers and routes, as well as "end - around - attacks"and transportation for guerrillas and partisans. Even submarines were even in service, on patrolling, screening, and providing clandestine transportation for raids along the coast.

In addition, the more than one hundred ships of the logistical support force provided supplies, replenished ships at sea, and transported the thousands of items, from gas to gaskets, necessary to fight a war.

WHAT IS THE "STATE VERSUS PEOPLE" THESIS?

This thesis is based on the belief there is a philosophical, if not psychological, difference between the institution of the nation - state and the people within that state. The question has to do with determining which of these is one's real enemy. War is considered the final political resolution of arguments between states, but when states mobilize their whole population, it is questionable just who or what one is fighting.

In some sense, wars have always been fought against nations rather than people. During World War II, it would be correct to say, most Americans saw the Nazi government as their enemy, not the German people. In the Pacific, however, the most common enemy was the Japanese. In Korea the distinction was even more difficult. We were allies of the Koreans and tended to see all Koreans as alike. Thus we put the face of the enemy on Kim Il Sung and his group. The enemy was the government.

There are several things to consider here. One has to do with the difference between the North Koreans and the Chinese in the eyes of those fighting them. The Chinese soldiers were seen as the primary enemy from the moment that they entered the war. They were respected and were considered more professional than the NKPA. They were also considered thought more humane to prisoners. However, there is evidence to suggest that in the Korean War, the real enemy was first of all the government of North Korea, the people of China, and the government of the Soviet Union.

The question of ends must be considered. One of the remarkable things about the Korean War is that confusion between state and people was so disorienting that little thought was given as to how to deal with it. Who was responsible? As it turned out, military people (who are often the last to know who the real enemy is) sought to end the war by focusing on the fighting forces, not the government.

WAS THE KATUSA PROGRAM EFFECTIVE?

That is a hard one to answer. The Korean Augmentation of the U.S. Army (KATUSA) program placed virtually untrained Koreans in American infantry divisions as replacements. (The program was also known as the Koreans Attached to the U.S. Army.) Often as many as three out of every seven men in an American unit were Korean soldiers. The idea was that they would learn on the job.

It is necessary to remember, even if it is unfortunate, that the American military was never particularly happy with the Koreans, especially the Korean military. Col. Harry G. Summers, who was there at the time, quotes Gen. John P. Hodges (the commander of the U.S. Armed Forces in Korea [USAFIK]) as saying that there were "only three things the troops in Japan are afraid of. They're gonorrhea, diarrhea and Korea." But reinforcements were needed, and in the beginning thirty to forty thousand young Korean men, sometimes recruited right off the street, were added to the depleted American Seventh, Twenty-Forth and Twenty-Fifth Infantry Divisions, and the First Cavalry Division. The effort to overcome the problems of language and lack of training by use of a buddy system was not totally successful. Most commanders eventually organized the KATUSA into separate units with their own officers.

However, as the war continued, the KATUSA improved, and they served many useful functions, including an important combat role. The South Korean government kept participation lower than the United States might have wanted, because the good conditions in American units made life in the ROK units appear even more difficult.

THE TERM "R AND R" USUALLY MEANS "REST AND RECUPERATION;" WHAT DOES THE TERM "REPLACEMENT AND ROTATION" MEAN?

During the Korean War, and especially when the armistice talks began, the military tested a policy of individual rotation of soldiers who has served a specific time. It was based on a point system. It assigned more points–as many as four per month–for those in combat zones, until a total of thirty-six was reached. The average combat soldier, if lucky, could expect to spend little more than a year in Korea, while someone in the rear might spend two years.

There were some obvious advantages. Soldiers had something to count on, in terms of return; it was easier on the troops than the World War II system, which tended to keep the same units in combat for long periods of time. On the down side was the fact that soldiers lost the unit identification and loyalty created by long-term assignments. The continual influx of "new men" also meant that units lost their most experienced men just as they were becoming ready for leadership and command roles. Also, it tended to create a class of "short-timers" who approached their duties with more caution than might otherwise have been the case.

This policy, which was to be carried on in Vietnam, was popular with the troops–though, as one can imagine, there were many complaints about the assignment of points.

WAS INCHON REALLY SUCH A REMARKABLE VICTORY?

The landing of United Nations troops at Inchon has to be considered a major military success, and certainly one of the most interesting amphibious landings ever conducted. While many of the stories about MacArthur's planning and the execution are more impressive than accurate, the fact is that it was a remarkable action.

It was originally conceived as Operation Bluehearts and scheduled for July 11, 1950; the desperate defense of Pusan forced General MacArthur to postpone it. MacArthur saw the landing as a bold move that would turn the tide in Korea, but to many, the risks were too great. Among the dangers were the extreme tides at the port of Inchon; the seawall in large segments of the landing area, sometimes as high as fifteen feet; the island of Wolmi-do, which sat in and guarded the harbor; the shortage of troops; and the fact that Eighth Army was still under considerable pressure.

MacArthur had every faith in the plan. The Joint Chiefs of Staff were not in favor of it, but they gave their approval, as did President Truman. The force MacArthur collected was powerful and experienced, but was accomplished while his command was under strength. Still, and despite the objections raised beforehand and questions about his later command, the landing at Inchon accomplished its purposes; it broke the pressure on Pusan, and led to a reversal of military fortunes in Korea.

The navy played a highly significant role, transporting, supporting, and softening up targets. Some 260 vessels were involved. The First Marine Division (minus the Marine Seventh Regiment, which was still en route) made the landing, it was quickly reinforced by the Seventh Infantry Division (Army) Gen. J. Lawton Collins, Army - Chief - of - Staff, said it was the masterpiece of one mind–MacArthur. "The loss of Seoul," he said, "doomed the entire North Korean People's Army." Lisle Rose writes, "Inchon was the last unambiguous U. S. military triumph for forty years,"[Rose 1999:223],a commentary on the transition then occurring in the character of war.

COMMENT

Today, after the passage of nearly half-a-century, there remain a lot of unanswered questions about the Korean War. Most of them have never been fully addressed, and more than a few have never been publicly raised. In the nature of the historical enterprise, the first step in the recording of past events lies in the development of a narrative. In 1999 new charges, this time of the death of civilians at No Gun Re, have been leveled against American troops. There are still so many areas for consideration. It is only after that need has been fulfilled that the historical community begins to seek out and address the smaller but highly important details of the event. It appears that the narrative period–which has been going on now for decades–has reached a peak and that scholars will soon begin to produce monographs dealing with more arcane aspects of the war.

Some questions, including some of those raised above, are so complex they will never be answered. As long as the Chinese Communist and North Korean archives remain closed, we will never have a good picture of the intentions of those nations. It is hard to imagine, given what we know, that they acted with the unanimity often ascribed to them. On the other hand, they shared a common goal–as did the United Nation–which gave them a united mission. It is the nature of communist governments to keep much of what they are thinking secret. Unlike democracies which tend to "tell it all," China has been very reserved about its intentions. This not only makes diplomacy difficult but it makes it very hard for a historian to understand what happens. Relations between North Korea and the United States have never been good, they do not seem to be getting any better, despite the time that has passed. We may never really know what Kim Il Sung was thinking, what his nation wanted, or how it reached the decision to fight its neighbor. Bruce Cumings has helped us understand some of this, but not all.

Finally, we must realize that some of the questions we ask in hope of answers are value–oriented. That is, these questions–and they are often the most important ones–are about beliefs. They, they will never be answered in any objective manner. In the final analysis, additional research and analysis can help us, but they cannot explain the vast differences in values represented by the nations involved. Military movement, even political implications, are often easier pinpoint than motives and intentions.

In war, as in so much human experience, what a person believes is affected by personal and institutional memories. Failure to understand intentions and behavior increases the possibility that a final understanding of the Korean War will be even more difficult to achieve than what we have learned so far.

Chapter 6

Leaders and Scoundrels

Someone in high authority will have to make up his
mind as to what is our goal.

Gen. Oliver Smith

Though hundreds of military men and women served in responsible positions during the Korean War, few, other than General of the Army Douglas A. MacArthur, are remembered. Certainly General MacArthur, heroic leader of World War I and World War II, as well as occupation commander of Japan, deserves to be remembered. But he is often remembered only at the cost of acknowledging the significant participation made by others.

But there were many who made a meaningful impact on the United Nations mission in Korea–a not just because they were dedicated soldiers, though most were. It was not just because they did their jobs in some incredible manner. Rather, they represent all those who, having been given a job, did it to the best of their ability. Some were leaders, one or two were scoundrels, but all provide interesting pictures of the war.

Obviously the selection of persons to be included in either category is arbitrary and subject to disagreement. Just as obviously, these people are all on the United Nations side; I have not chosen North Korean or Chinese leaders. These, appearing in no special order, are my selections.

LT. GENERAL WALTON HARRIS "BULLDOG" WALKER

General Walker rose to command Eighth Army in Korea by means of a career pattern typical for general officers. His assignments included the Meuse-Argonne campaign during World War I. In 1943 he accepted command of XX Corps, which was then assigned to Gen. George S. Patton's Third Army. After World War II, Walker was sent to Chicago to command Fifth Army. Then, in 1948, he was assigned to Japan to assume command of the Eighth U.S. Army.

When the Korean War broke out, General Walker had been ordered to take Eighth Army to the defense of South Korea. Pushed back by the North Korean troops, Walker held out along the Naktong River and at the Pusan perimeter. He managed to meet the many attacks by using the intricate railway system around Pusan to move his limited forces to the places of greatest stress. With the landing at Inchon in September 1950, Walker led Eighth Army in a successful breakout. He continued to push the increasingly demoralized and poorly supplied troops of the North Korean People's Army ahead of it, as he moved forward to join with X Corps.

His troops joined the invasion group for the attack on Seoul and the movement toward the 38th Parallel. When the decision was made to cross the 38th Parallel, Walker directed his troops in the capture of the North Korean capital and on north toward the Yalu River. More convinced than MacArthur of the presence of Chinese troops, he moved ahead more cautiously, limiting his extension, and when the Communist Chinese troops attacked he withdrew in remarkably good order. Retreating before the enemy, he evacuated his troops by sea from key harbors along the way. After about 130 miles, fight all the way, Gen. Walker was finally able to establish a line of defense south of the 38th Parallel.

General Walker, who had a reputation for reckless movement across land, was killed in a jeep accident at Uijongbu on December 23, 1950. Heading out he ordered his driver to pass a line of trucks. An ROK truck pulled out of line and hit the jeep; Walker died immediately. He was succeeded by Gen. Matthew B. Ridgway.

Walker was a brave and committed commander who had made a name for himself with General Patton. In many respects he seems to have followed in the footsteps of this flashy commander. Yet looking back, it is evident that he made some serious mistakes. Most, it seems in retrospect, were from failing to follow-up, or allowing the enemy to flank him. But, in his defense, General Walker was often the scapegoat for decisions made by other officers. The policies of the United States, as well as the individual command characteristics of General MacArthur, meant that he was not totally in command of the situation. During a significant part of his service, he was forced to fight with a divided command.

LT. GEN. MATTHEW BUNKER RIDGWAY

When the Korean War broke out, Lieutenant General Ridgway was the deputy chief of staff for plans. He was critical of how General MacArthur was running the war. Ridgway had been a division commander during World War II and had made a significant reputation as an airborne commander. He had served in a number of important staff assignments and was well respected as a strategist. He was named commander of Eighth Army following the death of General Walker. In taking this assignment, he was aware of the difficulties and concerned about General MacArthur's interference. It had been, however, MacArthur who asked for him.

When he arrived, he found the United Nations forces demoralized. It was Lt. Gen. Matthew B. Ridgway who was responsible for the later turnaround. He approached his job with an open and honest commitment, managing to bring new life into the defeated troops. Aware of the limitations of his command, Ridgway nevertheless began the process of rebuilding. He began with a general order to the troops about the reasons for the war. In the main, Ridgway stated, they were fighting because they were there; the only way out was to bring it to a close.

Ridgway also played a significant role in the decision to integrate the U.S. army, ordering the desegregation of Eighth Army. Ridgway developed the procedures to accomplish the integration of his command and convinced most of his commanders to push it as quickly as possible. He established a training schedule, provided the troops with showers and hot meals, and expanded the role of mobile hospital units. He replaced regimental commanders and older division commanders who "felt defeated," turning to younger officers with more aggressive attitudes. Thus by replacing some officers, taking a direct approach to the needs of the soldiers, and assuming an aggressive stand, Ridgway made Eighth Army ready to fight within a manner of weeks. As historian T. R. Fehrenbach describes it the Eighth U. S. Army "rose from it own ashes in a killing mood" [Fehrenbach 1963:3].

Ridgway approached his assignment in the belief that the most success could be achieved by aggressive action to produce the largest number of enemy casualties, rather than worrying over individual pieces of land. This system was effective, but was limited by the American tendency to a defensive policy.

When President Truman relieved General MacArthur from his duties as Far East commander, General Ridgway was assigned to replace him. Lt. Gen. James Van Fleet, who once commanded the 82nd Airborne Division, was named to the command of Eighth Army. Ridgway did not particularly like Van Fleet, but he respected his ability. On the other hand, he kept a great deal of control himself.

Ridgway was convinced that victory was almost impossible, and he seemed relieved when he was authorized to begin negotiations. Even during the negotiations, Ridgway pushed to maintain a territorial position. When General Eisenhower left NATO in Europe to return to the United States and politics, General Ridgway assumed the role of Supreme Commander Allied Powers Europe and the director of the North Atlantic Treaty Organization. General Mark Clark took over the Far East.

General Ridgway left Europe in October 1953 to become the U.S. Army Chief of Staff, a post in which he voiced some unpopular views. He would argue for maintaining the selective service, he was against opening the military academies to women, and he predicted the failure of an all-volunteer army. He was also an early, and outspoken, critic of American involvement in Vietnam.

There can be no doubt that General Ridgway saved the situation in Korea and, to the extent it was a victory, he made that victory possible. When he took command, on Christmas of 1950, Eighth Army was a defeated force on the point of collapse. Evacuation from Korean had been seriously considered. It was prevented, in large measure, by General Ridgway's ability, intelligence, experience, and personal courage.

Ridgway died on July 26, 1993, and is buried at Arlington Cemetery. He appears to have been a man created for the hour. While he had some difficulty staying out of the details of the operation of the war after he replaced MacArthur, he nevertheless was highly successful in the rejuvenation of Eighth Army. While in command, he maintained a strong and strategic presence as he worked through the early stages of the negotiation procedure.

MAJ. GEN. WILLIAM F. DEAN

General Dean was commissioned in the regular army as a second lieutenant in October of 1923. He rose to the rank of brigadier general in 1942 and major general in 1943. During World War II he was the commander of the 44th Infantry Division, where he won the Distinguished Service Cross for bravery.

Dean was appointed military governor of South Korea and held that position until the election of a republican government. He commanded the Seventh Infantry Division during its redeployment to Japan, and then he was appointed as chief of staff for the Eighth U.S. Army. After that, he was named commander of the 24th Infantry Division. It was the 24th that was selected to provide the first American presence in Korea. Major General Dean arrived to set up his headquarters on July 3, 1950. It was assumed that Dean's experience in South Korea, as well as his reputation as an aggressive leader, would produce the success needed. But, from the beginning he faced a much larger and far better trained enemy than anyone had expected.

His assignment was to hold the North Korean forces as long as possible. He managed to hold out, retreating slowly to the city of Taejon, losing 30 percent of his force. Never one to avoid a fight, General Dean was often with the troops at the front. Through this was good for morale, it sometimes prevented him from seeing the larger picture. Dean would later admit that he had been too close to the trees to see the forest.

It was a part of General Dean's personality to revert to his basic role as a foot soldier, and that he would acknowledge the difficulties that produced. He referred to himself as an "in-between general"–with no West Point ring, no World War I experience, and no service as an enlisted man. His division, committed in segments, finally gave way in the face of overwhelming odds, and while trying to escape, his party ran into an enemy patrol. Dean was forced to head for the hills. Separated from his men, he wandered for almost sixty days until captured by North Korean soldiers on August 25, 1950. General Dean was held prisoner, surviving the ordeal until his release on September 4, 1953, more than six weeks after the armistice was signed.

Concerned over the impact of his capture, General Dean returned to America to discover that the people saw him as a hero. He was awarded the Congressional Medal of Honor for his defense of Taejon. After his release he was assigned as deputy commander of the Sixth U.S. Army. General Dean published a narrative of his years as a prisoner, called simply *General Dean's Story* [1954]. He retired in 1955 and lived on the West Coast until his death on August 25, 1981.

A brave and competent officer, he was forced into fighting his part of the Korean War piecemeal; he never really had a chance to bring his division to bear. Perhaps more inclined to show rather than tell, he nevertheless became a symbol of the desperate nature of the country's early involvement. His years as a prisoner of the Chinese were hard years, and they kept him out of the main fighting of the Korean War.

ANNE WALLACE SUHR

When the Communists first took the capital city of Seoul, about sixty members of the Republic of Korea National Assembly remained behind. Toward the end of July, forty-eight of them held a meeting in which they expressed their allegiance to North Korea. At the meeting–and also swearing allegiance to the North Korean government–was an American who, voluntarily or not, ended up doing the wishes of the Communist government. Later called "Seoul City Sue," this Korean War version of "Tokyo Rose" broadcast appeals to American soldiers to surrender. She addressed them in an unmistakable American accent. Her name was Anne Wallace Suhr. She had come to Korea as a Methodist missionary. She later married a Korean national with strong leftist beliefs, which, in time, she adopted.

Never really much of a threat, she nevertheless added to the propaganda effort directed by the North Koreans. She is perhaps more interesting as an example of the many South Koreans, and citizens of other nations, who were inclined to side with the Communists once the war had been declared.

LT. GEN. GEORGE EDWARD STRATEMEYER

George Stratemeyer graduated from the U.S. Military Academy in 1915, a classmate of Omar Bradley. Stratemeyer transferred to the Army Air Corps in 1920 and commanded the Seventh Bombardment Group. When World War II broke out, he became commander of the Army Air Force in the China-Burma theater and remained in this command throughout the war. In April 1949 he was named Commanding General Far East Air Force, which consisted of the Fifth, 13th, and 20th Air Forces. He held this command when the Korean War began. He was a strong advocate of strategic bombing of industrial and communication targets, rather than the close air-ground support worked out so effectively by the Marine Air Wing. At the end of May 1950, General Stratemeyer had 1,172 planes and 33,625 men.

While he and General MacArthur disagreed on several issues, especially the extent of raids against the Yalu bridges, the air commander sided with MacArthur in favor of unlimited operations against Communist China. When he received his orders to bomb only the Korean side of the bridges, he declared, "It cannot be done–Washington must have known it cannot be done." He was also aware that the Communist Chinese would take full advantage of the restrictions placed on United Nations airborne harassment.

Lieutenant General Stratemeyer suffered a serious heart attack in May 1951 and relinquished his command to Lt. Gen. Otto P. Weyland. He retired from the Air Force in 1952 and died in August 1969.

He was a strong advocate of the Air Force, and respected as a commander who could get the most out of his men. The value of his services lay in his careful arrangement of attacks on North Korean airfields. His health prevented him from longer service in Korea, which might have revealed more of his overall strategy.

REAR ADM. JAMES H. DOYLE

Rear Admiral Doyle had learned his business during the amphibious landing at Guadalcanal. He was the commander of amphibious training for the Pacific Fleet when the Korean War broke out. It was his responsibility to arrange for and execute the landing of the 8th Cavalry Regiment, First Cavalry Division (Dismounted), on the beaches of Pohang–despite typhoon Helena.

Admiral Doyle understood the problems inherent in General MacArthur's plan to land at Inchon. But pushed for an answer at a meeting with the high command, he agreed that "Inchon is not impossible." Doyle was responsible for the development and execution of the plan, and he assumed command of naval forces at Inchon, watching the successful landing from his flagship USS *Mount McKinley*.

Later he assumed command of all naval activities and of all air activities within thirty-five miles of the evacuation fleet, which by the end of December took off more than a hundred thousand troops at Hungnam, in what S. L. A. Marshall called "the greatest fighting withdrawal of modern times." With 193 ships, he managed to save X Corps, its equipment, and many refugees. "They never put a glove on me," he reported. President Truman, hearing the news, called it his best Christmas present.

MAJ. GEN. CHARLES A. WILLOUGHBY

This interesting and highly controversial general had enlisted in the U.S. Army in 1910 as Adolph Charles Tscheppe-Weidenbach. His background is shrouded in mystery; his stories of his childhood varied, depending on to whom he was speaking. He won a commission in 1915, took a new name, and served in the Mexican border campaign and then in France during World War I. In the 1930s he was assigned as an instructor at the Command and General Staff College at Fort Leavenworth, Kansas. It was at the college that Willoughby met Gen. Douglas MacArthur. MacArthur was impressed, and when he accepted command in the Phillippines ,General Willoughby went with him.

In 1949, as a brigadier general and serving on General MacArthur's staff in Japan, Willoughby placed great faith in the more classical intelligence methods. He was inclined to discount many of the methods and intelligence gathering techniques developed during World War II.

As evidence mounted that the North Korean government was considering an attack, General Willoughby passed it on, but usually with an assessment discounting it. He was sure that there would be no civil war in Korea and no attack on the South. Even after the invasion Willoughby reported to the Pentagon that the fighting ability of the North Korean People's Army was a limited. During the fighting, General Willoughby continued to forward reports that, in essence, misled MacArthur and the Joint Chiefs of Staff. He was also not clear on the degree of confusion in the Republic of Korea Army and the deterioration of the South Korean government.

Out of touch with what was happening, he appeared to have an unlimited series of excuses to explain away events as they occurred. General Willoughby relied on the Nationalist Chinese for much of his intelligence information. He consistently underestimated the size of the North Korean, and then the Chinese, forces. He also seemed unaware of their ability, arguing that the North Koreans and Chinese had little or no combat experience. In fact, of course, many of the Communist troops had been at war for more than a decade.

What is especially difficult to understand is Willoughby's lack of intelligence data about the Chinese involvement–and his inability, even after they were involved, to get General MacArthur to take any action reflecting that knowledge. Willoughby's underestimation of the size of the enemy forces and overemphasis of the size of United Nations forces produced for field commanders false information upon which to base their actions.

A veteran of the campaigns at Bataan and Corregidor, he was a part of MacArthur's "Bataan Gang." He certainly was prone to protect MacArthur, even from knowledge that he should have had. Serving as G-2 (intelligence), he basked in the bright light of General MacArthur's headquarters. He was a powerful man, able to influence the intelligence picture. A challenge to General Willoughby was the same as a challenge to MacArthur. He gave the loyalty MacArthur demanded from his staff, probably to a fault. Close to MacArthur, he began to take on increasing power, and his views were highly influential throughout the Far East [Blair 1987:377].

Some observant critics have suggested that because General MacArthur did not want the Chinese to enter the war, Willoughby made it his job to convince everyone the Chinese were not involved. His wishful thinking was the source of faulty reasoning. While on occasion he would express concern over the role of the Chinese, he appeared determined to underestimate the number of Chinese opposing MacArthur. His suggestion of seventy thousand Chinese was a major underestimation [Marshall 1953:213]. He managed to dismiss X Corps's Chinese prisoners as "stragglers" or "volunteers" of no real significance.

Even in hindsight, it is hard to understand the intelligence chief and his strangely unfounded views. "Recent declaration by CCF leaders," he said about the Chinese warning that they would attack if the United States crossed the 38th Parallel, "is probably in the category of diplomatic blackmail" [Blair 1987:340]. Whether he actually falsified intelligence reports or was just too narrow minded and incompetent to maintain a reliable intelligence network is hard to know. Whichever was the case, he did not provide the supreme commander what he needed to fight the war and thus failed to do the job for which he had been selected.

Following MacArthur's removal, Major General Willoughby retired and became editor of the *Foreign Intelligence Digest.*

REAR ADM.WILLIAM G. ANDREWES

The Royal Navy responded almost immediately to the call of the United Nations for support. Adm. Sir Patrick Brind, RN, Commander in Chief (CinC), Far East Station, at Hong Kong radioed Adm. C. Turner Joy, Commander, Naval Forces Far East, that he could count on the ships of Task Group 96.8, located in south Japan, under Rear Adm. William G. Andrewes, KBE, CB, DSO, RN, second in command of the Far East Fleet. The task group consisted of Admiral Andrewes's flagship, the cruisers HMS *Belfast* and *Jamaica;* the carrier HMS *Triumph;* two destroyers, HMS *Cossack* and *Consort;* and three frigates, HMS *Black Swan, Alacrity,* and *Hart.*

Andrewes's group was assigned to the Blockade & Covering Force to conduct special reconnaissance missions and provide air cover for units of the Attack Force. His responsibility was complicated by the number of United Nations ships placed under his command by Admiral Joy. His job also included logistical support, the organization of the Japanese station and its personnel, and command and staff relations with British CinC. He was also assigned to specific interdiction missions, including the job of maintaining the naval blockade of the west coast of Korea.

He had under his control at one time the naval forces from Australia, Britain, Canada, Holland, France, Japan, Thailand, South Korea, and the United States. He was extremely successful in maintaining efficient relations, but he would once remark, "What we need now is the gift of tongues. Luckily we have no troops from Phrygia or Pamphilia" [Landsdown 1997:56].

The easy affiliation of American and British groups reflected the cooperation worked out during joint unit training. The task of controlling the sea lanes was divided between the East Coast Blockade Force and the West Coast Blockade Force. The eastern group was under Rear Adm. C. Hartman; the west coast group was under Rear Admiral Andrewes' s Task Force 96.53, later Korean Blockade Group 95.1. So sure was Andrewes's that the blockade was working, that he agreed to photograph every port and inlet on the west coast to corroborate that supplies were not coming in by sea. It is doubtful his force was able by late summer 1950 to stop supplies, but it is certain that he managed to slow them down considerably.

Critical of the value of unspotted naval gunfire, Admiral Andrewes commented that apart from the morale and psychological value to the United Nations troops and the challenge to the Communists, "it is of little real value, and many thousands of shells must have fallen harmlessly on the barren hills and rocks along the east coast of Korea" [Cagle 1957:31].

Admiral Andrewes's command was involved in the landing at Inchon. At the end of the Chromite operation General MacArthur signaled him, "My heartfelt felicitations on the splendid conduct of the Fleet under your command" [Landsdown 1997:47]. Andrewes himself had less flourish: "The absence of the spectacular is a measure of the complete success achieved." During the retreat from the Yalu, Andrewes and his force were involved in several evacuation, the most significant of them the withdrawal of Eighth Army troops at Chinnampo.

On January 1, 1951, William G. Andrewes was knighted and promoted to vice admiral. For the next six weeks he served under an American rear admiral; on February 12 Vice Admiral Andrewes was made task force commander. At that point there was a reversal of command and deputy roles. On April 3, 1951, Andrewes departed from the area.

VICE ADM. CHARLES TURNER JOY

When the war broke out Vice Admiral Joy was Commander Naval Forces, Far East. He had available one cruiser, the USS *Juneau*; four destroyers, the USS *De Haven, Mansfield, Lyman K. Swenson*, and *Collett*; and six minesweepers. During World War I he had served on the USS *Pennsylvania*, and during the interwar period with the USS *Yangtze*. During World War II he commanded the cruiser USS *Louisville*. On August 26, 1949, he was assigned as Commander, Naval Forces Far East, and was serving there when the Korean War broke out.

He felt that the United States should be involved in an effort to stop the North Korean advance but admitted that he "didn't think we would. Consequently, when the United Nations took action, and the American forces were ordered into Korea, I was quite surprised [and] General MacArthur was likewise surprised [and as a] consequence we had no plans for this type of war" [Cagle 1957:31].

Despite the surprise, the United States Navy moved to support the transfer of supplies from Japan, and it was quickly called upon to provide naval forces in direct support of the retreating troops. "It is not an exaggeration," Admiral Joy would say later, "that without the Navy the Pusan perimeter could never have been held."

When it came time to begin negotiations with the Communists, at 1000 hours on 10 July 1952, Admiral Joy was assigned as the chief of the United Nations delegation. His deputy was Adm. Arleigh Burke. In May 1952, after ten months of negotiations, he was succeeded as head of the truce team by Maj. Gen. William K. Harrison Jr. In June, after nearly three years, he turned the Naval Forces, Far East Command, over to Vice Adm. Robert P. Briscoe.

On his departure Admiral Joy provided the following insights, first on preparation and second on negotiations:

The Korean War may not go down in history as a major war or as a war that appreciably changed the maps of the world. But it nevertheless is a war of deep significance. It has been a war to prevent a larger war by serving notice on a ruthless enemy that he can go so far and no further. From the standpoint of national preparedness we have been awakened to the danger that surrounds us. Let us hope that we remain awake.

If there are still those in the Free World who believe that the enemy can be moved by logic, or that he is susceptible to moral appeal, or that he is willing to act in good faith, those remaining few should immediately disabuse themselves of that notion. It was a mistake to assume, or even hope, that the enemy was capable of acting in good faith [Biskind 1983:439].

Admiral Joy returned in 1952 to become the superintendent of the U.S. Naval Academy. He retired in July of 1954 and died on June 13, 1956. His name and contribution were honored by the christening of a new destroyer USS *Turner Joy*.

MARGUERITE "MAGGIE" HIGGINS

Among the first war correspondents who flew into Kimpo airfield at the outbreak of the Korean War, was "Maggie" Higgins, a reporter for the *New York Herald Tribune*. How she got her assignment is one of the more interesting stories of the emerging feminist movement, but she was already well known for her aggressive journalism. She was young, feisty, and more than willing to use her charm to get what she wanted. She landed into the heat of battle; on her arrival the area was under fire and two planes were burning at the far end of the field. She moved with the few Americans of the Korean Military Assistance Group who were still in support of the South Koreans—learning, as she would later report, a new interpretation for KMAG: Kiss My Ass Goodby. Retreating with the army, she was nevertheless able to file a June 28 report on the routing of the South Korean government and the premature destruction of the Han River Bridge. She managed to join survivors who were rowed across the river and then walked with the retreating troops to Suwon.

Higgins radiated confidence and even in the retreat was optimistic. Following the retreat she returned to Tokyo aboard the *Bataan* with General MacArthur. She then provided an early *Saturday Evening Post* article on what was happening. The army told her to depart, believing it was no place for a woman to be gallivanting around. She often felt her path was blocked and that her requests were ignored because she was a woman in a "man's business." She was rather consistently expelled from one dangerous situation after another. Certainly there was danger, of course; during the Korean War ten war correspondents were killed. It is probably true, however, that she was restricted where men were not. Yet it is also true that she was difficult at times, taking advantage whenever she could. She was, beyond a doubt, brave and determined to get the story. General MacArthur seemed to like her, even though he would order her out on occasion as he became increasingly afraid of press leaks.

For a long time she was credited with announcing the first American battle death, but that later proved to be false. She did, however, manage to file some excellent stories, often despite official challenges. In her news articles she reported on the Red aggression, the role of the media in the war, and her increasing disagreement with the military. She was outspoken in her views, writing on one occasion: "It is a mockery for Truman to tell the nation that three and a half million soldiers can protect us when every responsible soldier knows that it will be closer to fourteen million if we want to win." She was direct in her indictment and criticism of American unpreparedness [Kerin 1994:222-223].

Her interpretations were dramatic and her descriptions of battle more cinematic than accurate. She wrote at Inchon, "The yellow glow [the sun] that cast over the green-clad marines produced a technicolor splendor that Hollywood could not have matched" [Guttman 1967:145]. She showed up in Hagaru-ri on December 5, 1950, as American troops were beginning the evacuation. She was known, as well, for her outspokenness. She asked one wounded GI on the Chosin retreat, what had been the most difficult thing he had done: "To get a three-inch prick out of six inches of clothing," he replied [Higgins 1951:230].

As the situation grew worse and most of the correspondents were forced out, she was flown to Tokyo. She became increasingly critical of America's unpreparedness. After leaving Korea, the able young woman wrote a book, *War in Korea: The Report of a Woman Combat Correspondent* [1951], which provided a vivid illustration of the difficulties of war. Her contribution in opening the way for other women correspondents has not been fully acknowledged.

LT. EUGENE FRANKLIN CLARK

Lieutenant Clark played a rather unique role in the invasion of Inchon. Clark, a chief-yeoman during the Pacific War, had commanded an LST and later the USS *Errol,* an attack transport. He had served as the chief interpreter-translator for the war crimes hearings on Guam. Transferred to G-2 (intelligence) on General MacArthur's Tokyo staff, he accepted a special reconnaissance mission.

The planning for the invasion at Inchon required exact information about tides. The Japanese maps disagreed with earlier United States surveys. A great deal of topographical and weather information about the area had already been collected by Lt. Cdr. Ham Myong Su (ROKN). Clark was to get the additional data needed to resolve the ambiguity. He was also to be in charge of a group of South Korean agents–known as "line-crossers"–who would scout the Inchon area to see if any anti-invasion measures were being taken.

After a briefing by Vice Admiral Andrewes, RN, who was in charge of the blockade, Clark and his team boarded the British destroyer HMS *Charity.* As they drew nearer to their destination, they were taken aboard the ROK frigate *PC-703.* Clark and his two companions were landed on the small island of Yonghung -do on September 1, 1950. The island was located at a strategic spot about fifteen miles below the port of Inchon.

Clark had with him a radio, two machine guns, and a few small arms. He also had the only motorized sampan on the island. The island itself was small, no more than four miles wide and six miles in length. The islanders were

friendly and aided in setting up a defense against the nearby occupied island of
Tabu-do. Clark organized a group of coastwatchers from among the islanders.
A good portion of these investigators were teenage boys, but a few were older
men from the village. He sent them out on missions to collect as much
information as possible before the invasion.

Clark personally investigated the harbor, actually measuring the sea walls and
identifying high and low tide: a range of from twenty-nine to thirty-six feet, as
well as a current of five knots. The mud flats were so deep that a man in
fighting gear could sink up to the waist. Using a one-time-code-pad, Clark
reported that the Japanese maps were the more accurate of those available. He
also discovered that the island of Wolmi-do had more gun emplacements and
was better defended than the Navy had expected, and that Fish Channel was
heavy mined.

Clark's small band was very active. Between the officer and his agents, more
than thirty small vessels, most carrying civilians, were captured. One evening
more than sixty North Korean soldiers waded across from a nearby island in an
attempt to dislodge them, but Clark and his force drove them back. Using his
radio Clark called in bombers which managed to discouraged any further
harassment.

About four miles east of the island, and observable from Yonghung - do, was
the small island of Palmi-do, where the East and Flying Fish Channels joined.
On one of his night surveys, Clark discovered that the old French lighthouse on
Palmi-do could be fixed. He radioed Tokyo that he would do his best to light the
old oil lamp on the night the bombardment vessels headed into the channel.

In the early hours of September 14, 1950, as the warships began the
navigation of Flying Fish Channel, they found the job made easier by the light
shining from atop Palmi - do. Lieutenant Clark, wrapped in a blanket, watched
the invasion from the small island. Later Eugene Clark was awarded the Navy
Cross.

LT. DAVID H. SWENSON

Gun Fire Support Group 6, an international collection of vessels, headed up
Flying Fish Channel in the effort to neutralize Wolmi-do. It was the first step
in the invasion of Inchon. Their fire mission was to begin at 0700 on September
13, 1950. Return fire from the Communist batteries hit the USS *Gurke*. Then
the USS *Collet* was hit twice, wounding two men. The USS *Lyman K. Swenson*
suffered a near miss. However, fragments from the explosion hit and instantly
killed Lt. (j.g.)David H. Swenson, the only death of the Wolmi-do bombardment.
It also wounded Ens. John N. Noonam. Ironically, Lieutenant Swenson was the
nephew of the man for whom the destroyer was named: Capt. Lyman K.
Swenson had been lost with his ship, the cruiser USS *Juneau,* during World War
II. This was the first USS *Juneau,* sunk at the Battle of Guadalcanal; the five
Sullivan brothers had been among those lost.

Dave Swenson had a promising career. He had been the brigade commander at the Academy, the highest cadet rank, and stood second in his class academically. At 0800, before it moved up Flying Fish Channel, the advance force stopped and, with the British and American flags at half-mast, the cruiser USS *Toledo* buried Lieutenant Swenson at sea. A marine guard of honor fired three volleys.

Chapter 7

Operations

Designed to meet abnormal military inhibitions, our strategic plan
involved constant movement to keep the enemy off balance.

Gen. Matthew Ridgway

Americans have a long tradition of commemoration. They have acknowledged
the massive and essential battles in which Americans have tested their
principles and their personal honor. Through a long and often violent history,
many such national tests come to mind: Lexington, Concord Bridge,
Yorktown, the Battle of Lake Erie, Antietam, Gettysburg, Guantanamo,
Meuse-Argonne, the Battle of Leyte Gulf, the Battle of the Bulge, Hamburger
Hill.

Many highly significant battles were fought in the Korean War. Perhaps the
battle most remembered is Chosin, a major defeat. Acknowledging the Korean
War properly will require considerable study of many of the other
engagements, like Chipyong-ni, Gloucester Hill, Kunu-ri, and the Naktong
Perimeter. There also needs to be further analysis of the prolonged hill war
that so typified the fighting in Korea.

In addition to specific battles, the military is often called upon to focus its
resources and personnel on particular targets or project. These efforts were
often given names reflective of the missions involved. Some operations had
immediate combat goals, others were long-term efforts or even national
politics. The following twenty-one operations reflect of some of the
significant, and highly interesting, special missions of the Korean War.

OPERATION ALBANY

By November 1950, Eighth Army had captured, and was holding, several
thousands of prisoners of war. This was many more prisoners than had been
anticipated. The United Nations Command was pushed to the limit to provide
troops for the advance toward the Yalu River; there were few troops available
to guard the prisoners securely. Nor were there people available to provide care

for them. The internal needs of the hasty and temporary camps were often left to the prisoners themselves. The guards were forced to rely on the prisoners cooperation for discipline and for the distribution of supplies. The guards rarely entered the camps themselves.

Following the Chinese intervention in the Korean War, Gen. Matthew B. Ridgway became concerned with the large numbers of unsupervised POWs in his midst. They could, under the right conditions, be mobilized as a powerful force against him. Thus, in the spring of 1951, Operation Albany was set in motion. Ridgway ordered the removal of most of the POWs, scattered in camps all over Korea, and relocated them on the island of Koje-do, about twenty miles off Pusan, where a large, though rough, POW camp had been developed

The conditions in all the POW camps were very poor, and as prisoners arrived in far larger numbers than expected, things got worse. As many as two thousand men and women a day were brought into the camp in the first few months after the operation began. Koje-do would later prove a major discipline and control problem.

OPERATION BLUEHEARTS

Shortly after the war began, General Douglas MacArthur flew to Korea to take a first hand look at what was happening. Standing on a hill overlooking the retreating forces, MacArthur envisioned a plan to save South Korea in one grand stroke. The plan was reminiscent of, and probably inspired by, Gen. James Wolfe's successful landing at Quebec in 1759. MacArthur projected that an invasion force could be delivered on the west coast of Korea, near Inchon. From there the United Nations could cut the North Korea lines of supply and communication, and strike at Seoul, thereby reducing, the pressure on the Pusan perimeter. He wanted the amphibious action to take place on July 22, 1950, just eighteen days after the plan was announced to the staff.

MacArthur envisioned the use of the U.S. First Cavalry Division, an engineering battalion, and a marine regimental combat team. It would be a classic move. But the troops that MacArthur planned to use were needed elsewhere. The North Korean People's Army was pushing its attack at numerous points on the Pusan perimeter. General Walker needed all available resources to prevent the United Nations forces from being driven into the sea.

Because of the desperate situation, General MacArthur postponed his plan, but he did not kill it. It was later to be resurrected as Operation Cromite, the invasion of Inchon.

OPERATION CLAM UP

By November 1951 the character of military action in Korea was being described as an "active defense strategy." On November 12, General Ridgway sent a directive to his subordinate commanders ordering that they take no aggressive ground action. A cease-fire line had been presented as a part of the armistice plan, and if accepted, it would run along the demarcation line.

When the Communists allowed the thirty-day limit to expire on the proposal, the United Nations Command had few offensive plans ready. Operation Clam Up was set in motion between February 10 and 15, 1952. It was designed to capture a large number of the enemies. The idea was to convince the Communist troops on line that the United Nations had withdrawn. To support this assumption, all air strikes, artillery fire, and ground patrols were discontinued. The hope was that the Chinese and North Korean commanders would send out reconnaissance patrols to see what was happening, and that significant numbers of them would be captured.

The Communists, however, either did not notice the silence or failed to draw the desired conclusions. Rather, they used the time to reinforce their defensive positions. The whole idea, like so many things tried by the United Nations during this period, appears to have been just one more effort to end the frustrating stalemate that had developed along the front.

OPERATION CHEERFUL

In December of 1951, the Chinese took the islands of Ung-do and Chongyong. The Canadians were given the responsibility for retaking them. In a planning meeting it was decided to launch a two-pronged attack, which, in honor of the Christmas season, was called Operation Cheerful. The idea was to attack the islands simultaneously, using the combined forces of UN guerilla units known as Leopard and Salamander. This was the first of many mistakes that were made. The partisans were sabotage experts and they could live off the land for days while destroying facilities behind enemy lines. But they had little or no experience with frontal attacks. Besides, the two groups had never worked together, they reported to different commanders, and they operated without conventional discipline.

The Canadian naval units assigned to the attack provided a full - scale naval bombardment. It began at 1800 hours as four towed junks headed for the islands. As the junks closed in on the targets, one of the began to take on water. The guerrillas, apparently having a change of mind about the attack, sank the boat. This cut the force available for the Ung-do attack.

When the remaining troops landed, there was considerable opposition. One mortar round sank another junk. Command elements aboard the Canadian destroyer *Cayuga* took charge and ordered minesweepers to evacuate the guerrillas. A few of the guerillas boarded one of the remaining junks and immediately left. The Canadians followed but decided against firing on it. The operation failed to accomplish its mission.

OPERATION (PLAN) CHOW CHOW

Once the last American occupation forces had moved out of Korea in the

1940s, the best that President Rhee could hope for was that Americans were willing to return in case of an attack from the North. It turned out, however, that the contingency plans drawn up for General MacArthur contained no such option. As the troops withdrew, MacArthur gave up all military command in Korea. It had already been determined that an American commitment would place unreasonable demands on limited military and economic resources and might draw the United States into an undeclared war in Asia.

But some plans were made for American action from Japan. The part of the plan that related to Korea, named Chow Chow, was drawn up in July 1949. It called for MacArthur's Far East Command to evacuate all American civilian and military personnel, as well as some specifically identified foreign nationals. The plan called for Far East Command to respond in any general emergency, but it recognized that if hostilities broke out between the United States and the Soviet Union, the Americans in South Korea would have to fend for themselves. The plan envisioned no scenario in which American troops would be called upon for ground action in South Korea.

OPERATION DECOY

Following the success at Inchon, the United Nations used the threat of further amphibious landings to frighten the Communists into committing troops to the defense of the threatened area. There were several threats. One major effort was called Operation Decoy. The operational order called for a regimental combat team to seize by amphibious assault, occupy, and defend a beachhead in the Kojo area. The purpose was twofold. The first goal was to create a psychological reaction among enemy troops that would give the United Nations an advantage. A second purpose was to draw enemy reinforcements from outlying areas to defend the area. The command believed that the siege at Wonsan had kept troops tied down and hoped was the danger of another attack would serve the same purpose.

The interesting fact is that the operation order did not mention that the amphibious evolution was a deception. The value of the operation lay in surprise, and those in command were taking no chances. The forces involved, from minesweepers to aircraft carriers, were not aware of the true purpose of the operation, which was scheduled for October 15, 1952. Gen. Mark Clark approved the operation, and Vice Adm. Joseph J. Clark was the commander of Joint Task Force 7.

Ships headed for their assigned position on October 1, and Task Group 76.4, carrying troops, left for the area on October 9. On October 14 the flagship, USS *Iowa.* joined the bombardment. On board the transports reveille was held at 0300, but heavy fog prevented disembarkation. Later in the day, when most of the fog had lifted, boats began their run for the shore. Then at a prearranged point, they stopped, about five thousand yards from the beach. On their return they were picked up by the transports. Shortly after, the operation was declared to have been an exercise.

The exercise may have provided some necessary rehearsal but it did little to draw enemy troops. Later intelligence reported that the enemy had withdrawn from the shore positions and no new troops appear to have been brought in, at least none apparently motivated by the threat of an American attack. Ten enemies were reported killed by an air attack.

OPERATION EVERREADY

This was a plan to save us from our friends. It was developed to block any effort by South Korean President Syngman Rhee to interfere with the execution of the war or to prevent a final armistice. Rhee was determined that the war would not end. He wanted no agreement that failed to force the withdrawal of all Chinese troops from Korea and the total disarmament of North Korea.

Operation Everready, planned by Eighth Army, would be set in motion if the ROK troops did not respond to United Nations directives, if President Rhee and his government tried to take an independent route, or if ROK troops became hostile.

In case of the first or third possibilities, Eighth Army was to disarm the hostile ROK troops and hold them in check. But if Rhee and his government tried to follow an independent line, Eighth Army would conduct a military coup. They would proclaim martial law, seize the dissenting government leaders, and set up a government under someone who would be cooperative.

American policy makers were willing to accept a series of defensive agreements or mutual pacts, but they did not want to replace Rhee with a military government. Even though President Rhee appeared to be supporting the armistice efforts, the plan was updated and sent to Washington for approval. This time it directed that the United Nations Command would withdraw all logistical support, cut off power sources to the capital, blockade the South Korean coast, or if necessary, use ROK soldiers against their own government.

When Rhee threw a wrench into the slowly grinding gears of negotiations by his release of more than twenty-five thousand POWs, the new Eisenhower administration chose to negotiate with him. Eventually, on consideration of a mutual defense treaty and major economic aid, Syngman Rhee allowed the armistice to be signed without further trouble.

OPERATION GLORY

The armistice agreement was stalled for a long time by problems created by an exchange of prisoners. But even after that was worked out, one other question remained, a question that was nearly as touchy as the exchange of POWs. This had to do with the location and exchange of war dead. In the end the initial exchange worked out.

Many United Nations soldiers had fallen in areas that, following the armistice, were either in the DMZ or behind enemy lines. Several POWs had died in captivity and were buried in camp cemeteries. Operation Glory was the program conducted after the armistice to locate and exchange the bodies of those who had died in the conflict. Despite these efforts, the remains of many fallen soldiers were never located.

OPERATION HUDSON HARBOR

The atomic bomb, with all its horror, hung over the Korean War as a potential but undesired weapon. The possibility that the United States would use atomic weapons increased when the United Nations suffered major defeats, particularly following the Chinese spring offensive of 1951. To deal with the question of using nuclear weapons a special project known as Operation Hudson Harbor was established. The overriding concern was over how the war might be brought to a close: a prolonged war with China, given its massive manpower reserves, would make the idea of using an atomic bomb more acceptable. The concept was really quite simple. The more complex problem was how the war might be brought to a conclusion without the bomb but also without a major loss of either ground troops or aircraft.

On May 31, 1950, General Ridgway urged the use of the atomic bomb and asked that thirty be sent to Korean for possible deployment. As early as June 1951, Gen. J. Lawton Collins, U.S. Army Chief of Staff, produced a plan for the use of atomic weapons in Korea. He urged the identification of targets and as a series of practice raids against North Korean targets. The Joint Chiefs of Staff approved the plan, on the basis that the atomic weapons would be used only in the event Eighth Army was in danger of being pushed into the sea. President Truman gave his approval, and practice raids began, starting in September, and under extreme secrecy, a series of practical experiments were carried out with dummy bombs, designed to anticipate the effects of real ones.

In April 1953, the Communists once again threatened to boycott the peace talks. In response, Eisenhower approved a plan submitted to him, National Security Council Document 147, a plan was to authorize nuclear attacks on Chinese air bases, supplies, and transportation forces was suggested to bring the North Korean and Chinese Communists back to the bargaining table. Either the threat worked or the Chinese had decided to bring the war to an end, because they returned, apparently more interested in working something out.

OPERATION INSOMNIA

For many military leaders, the key to victory in Korea lay in cutting off the North Korean and Chinese front from its source of supply. Overall, efforts in that direction were not very successful. No matter how well the United Nations hit supply centers, cut railway lines, and destroyed trucks and wagons, the

Communists rebuilt. The supplies continued to roll despite the disruptions. Operation Insomnia was but one of several attempts. Pilots had observed that Communist supply trucks would leave supply depots just as interdiction flights of interdiction were ending. The pilots inferred that after several months of experience, the enemy was holding supply columns back until after the nightly raids had been completed.

Operation Insomnia, which began on May 13, 1952, was an effort to counter this procedure, by launching planes at midnight for the night raid, and again at 0200 to catch the late - leaving trucks. The hope was that when the midnight raid was over, the Communists would send trucks out on their nightly journey, and to be hit by the second wave of night bombers.

The operation ran until June 9, 1952. The general agreement was that the operation had accomplished little other, than harassment.

OPERATION STRANGLE

Special other special efforts were made to restrict the flow of supplies to Communist troops. One of the more concentrated of these was Operational Strangle, from June 5 to September 20, 1951.

The plan was to establish a line across Korea at which the Chinese were engaged, and then divide the area north of it into designated target areas for the various air units. The idea was to focus attacks on supply routes in an effort to slow, or prevent, movement of supplies along them. A one-degree wide strip was drawn across the neck of North Korea, and eight attack areas were identified. Planes from the First Marine Aircraft Wing would be responsible for three eastern routes; the Fifth Air Force in Korea was assigned the three western areas, and the carriers of Task Force 77 were given the responsibility for the two central areas. Sites within each area were identified. that, if destroyed, the theory was, would create a stranglehold on the Communists forces. The attacks consisted of direct bombing and strafing, and night illumination with night bombing. In an effort to slow repairs, delayed-action bombs were dropped, with leaflets scattered to warn the repair crews of the danger.

At the completion of the first two weeks, the results were disappointing.; the raids had not stopped the supplies as expected. But the raids continued. It finally became apparent that the program was not going to work. Bomb craters did not stop highway traffic, and the limited number of breaks caused in rail lines could be, and generally were, fixed within a few hours.

What was called Operation Strangle was an embarrassing failure. The failure brings into serious question the long-held belief that the air war in Korea was successful, and that to a large degree, it was air superiority that won the war for the United Nations. It also provides an example of the costly nature of the war. The Communists responded with a surprising increase in anti-aircraft fire. The defense was so effective that one of the routes through which the navy was to fly was nicknamed "death row." In a military sense, as an economic one, the risk and loss of a million-dollar plane, and an equally expensive pilot, to disrupt rail traffic for two or three hours was not wise.

A last-case adjustment was made, to select key points and then destroy them with bombs. It was called Operation Saturate and, no more effective than Operation Strangle, it lasted only a short time. It ended in late May.

OPERATION KILLER

When Ridgway took command of Eighth Army, morale was low, and the military initiative had been lost. One of the steps he took to reverse the situation was the launching on February 21, 1951, of Operation Killer.

The plan was fairly simple. Operation Order 14 called for the First Marine Division to attack to the northeast, supported by IX Corps. This force included the Commonwealth Division, the First Cavalry, and the 24th Infantry Division. X Corps, with the ROK Third, and Fifth Divisions, and the United States Second, Seventh Infantry Divisions, were on the right. To the west, I Corps, including the First ROK Division and the American 25th Infantry Division, was to hold the Han River at Line Boston. The 187th Airborne Regimental Combat Team was held in reserve. The advance involved about a hundred thousand men.

The primary purpose of this operation, as the name implies, was to inflict as much damage possible—that is, to kill as many enemy soldiers and destroy as much of the enemy's equipment as possible. To accomplish this the United Nations units moved forward in a coordinated front all alone the line, being particularly careful to avoid effort by the Chinese to interdict.

As was his custom, MacArthur released news of the operation to the press suggesting that he had been responsible for the new initiative. Actually, his involvement had been minor. He was impressed enough with its success, however, to arrange to be in Korea in fact, it was his last trip to Korea as Far East Commander—when Ridgway unleashed the next effort, Operation Ripper.

The rain and early melting snow made it very difficult to advance. The North Korean soldiers seemed to melt before the advancing troops. At the conclusion of the attack Operation Killer had not destroyed the large number of the enemy soldiers anticipated. But despite this failure, the whole operation probably should be considered a success. The aggressive action helped to form the United Nations line and moved the Eighth Army into a major initiative. It expanded General Ridgway's reputation and, in turn, greatly enriched the General's appreciation of the Marine Corps.

Because of the negative nature of the publicity surrounding the names "killer" and "ripper," General Ridgway was asked to consider somewhat less aggressive names for his operations. Ridgway expressed dismay that people did not want to admit what they were trying to do, that is, to kill enemy soldiers. However his aggressive operations were thereafter identified by the code word "courageous."

OPERATION LEE

This operation was named after its commander, the captain of the ROK
naval patrol craft, *Kum Kang San* (PC 702). The plan was an attack on the
Tokchok Islands, to capture and occupy them for use in future intelligence
gathering. A month before the successful invasion at Inchon, and with no
knowledge of that plan, Lee's unit–10 men supported by two YMS–went
ashore on August 17, 1950. On the following day, with the help of the
Canadian destroyer HMCS *Athabaskan,* they secured the island. The men of
Operation Lee landed on the channel approach island of Yonghung Do on the
19th, and then moved along the coastal islands. On the 20th, Operation Lee
destroyed the radio gear at the lighthouse at Palmi-do in Inchon Harbor.
During the operation considerable intelligence information was collected
ROK lieutenant commander Ham Mysong Su.

Beside the occupation of essential territory, the primary effect was to weaken
the North Korean forces at Inchon. As the planners had hoped, the troops of
the North Korean People's Army, fearing further attacks, had sent troops
southwest in response to Lee's operation. The operation continued until
October 2, 1950.

OPERATION LITTLE SWITCH

After months of negotiation, the Communist Chinese agreed to the exchange
of sick and wounded prisoners. The exchange had been suggested by Gen.
Mark Clark, and when authorized to do so he broadcast his willingness to
begin discussions. Toward the end of March, the Communists command
indicated a willingness to discuss the issue. The two sides went to the table and
worked out an agreement.

At this point, the Americans were still insisting on voluntary repatriation.
They agreed, however, to give the terms "sick" and "wounded" very broad
interpretations. An agreement was reached by April 11, 1953, which given the
nature of the armistice talks, was accomplished with incredible speed. Between
April 20 and May 3, 1953, under elaborate security the United Nations,
Communist Chinese, and North Korea exchanged sick and wounded prisoners.
The Americans called it Operation Little Switch.

The exchange of prisoners lasted until the 3d of May. During the process, the
United Nations turned over more than 6,670 Communists prisoners, including
5,194 North Koreans, 1,030 Chinese and 446 civilians. The Communists
released 684 prisoners, ninety-four on litters. Of these 149 were American,
471 South Koreans, thirty-two British, fifteen Turks, six Colombians, five
Australians, two Canadians, and one each from the Philippines, Greece, the
Netherlands, and South Africa.

A rather extensive "survey" was conducted among the American forces. It uncovered some rather diverse stories of mistreatment, both mental and physical. But perhaps more important was the belief, by some American authorities, that some of the returned American prisoners had been "brainwashed" during their imprisonment. The military were asked to separate those who were suspected of being pro-Communist and send them back to the United States in isolation. General Clark refused. Almost all of the 143 Americans who were returned had been wounded or very ill, but most returned in reasonably good health.

OPERATION MOOLAH

The appearance of the Russian-made MiG over the Korean skies came as something of a shock. There was great interest in the plane which had some significantly advanced features. The United States wanted to see a MiG up close and in friendly hands, so it could be studied. Late in the war, on March 20, 1953, the Joint Chiefs of Staff offered a prize of a hundred thousand dollars and political asylum to the first MiG pilot who landed a plane at Kimpo, near Seoul. They also provided a fifty thousand dollar reward for each additional pilot. The Air Force set aside $250,000 for this purpose. In April. thousands of leaflets announcing this award were dropped along the Yalu River and broadcast in Russian, Chinese, and Korean.

There were two theories behind this decision. One was that the offer would serve as a psychological weapon during the armistice talks; the reward might cause some insecurity among Russian military leaders. More important, however, was the hope that the United States could get its hands on a MiG in good condition, an. The idea that had emerged from the Harvard Russian Research Center. On July 9, 1951, a Chinese pilot ejected and allowed his damaged MiG to crash onto a sandbar off the coast. Operation MiG was launched by the United Nations to recover the wreck; it succeeded on July 20 and 21, despite heavy enemy bombardment to prevent the recovery. The pieces were flown to the United States, but the Air Force still wanted an operational machine.

There is some evidence that the Chinese limited the number of fighters sent out during a short period following the announcement. Apparently the authorities wanted to recheck the loyalty of their pilots. But the ploy did not work as the American's expected. It was not until well after the armistice, on September 21, 1953, that a MiG was delivered. Claiming that he was not aware of the award and that he was seeking only political asylum, North Korean Air Force lieutenant No Kom-sok landed a MiG at Kimpo.

The acquisition was considered very valuable, but the defector did not receive his money from the government. There appeared to be some concern about how it "looked," and so other arrangements were made. A CIA front eventually provided the North Korean pilot with an equal reward in cash, education, and vocational opportunities.

OPERATION RATKILLER

The movement of troops and the occupation of territory were hampered by the existence of large and well equipped Communist guerrilla units. In an effort to establish some sort of control over these harassing forces, the South Korean government declared martial law in the southwestern part of the Chirisan Mountain region.

A task force was created and named after its commander, Maj. Gen. Paik Sun Yup. Task Force Paik managed to cut off the communications and movement into the restricted area. To wrap up the exercise, Operation Ratkiller was established. It was an antiguerilla pincer movement that operated along a perimeter 163 miles in length. The ROK Eighth Division came in from the southwest. With the Capital Division from the northwest and the National Police covering the gap, the squeeze began. The operation was conducted in three phases, December 1-4, December 19-January 4, and from the 6 to the 31st of January. A mop-up activity operated until March 15, 1953

The effort was successful in that it caught or killed a reported 19,000. That figure seems high, and Ridgway's estimate was less than 10,000. But regardless of the number it did provide some relief, albeit temporary, from guerrilla operations in the area.

OPERATION SQUEEGEE

In May of 1951 the Canadian ship *Nootka* was among the escort and bombardment task force. Her particular assignment was the destruction of transportation and communications facilities. Members of the crew took particular interest in destroying bridges. But luck had not been with them. They had managed to close several tunnels, had torn up a good number of rail way lines, and achieved hits on numerous bunkers. But one bridge, located just south of Sonjin, and called "the Rubber Bridge," was the greatest failure. It had achieved its name because, even after the most desperate shelling, the bridge always remained in tact. It became a personal issue with the crew.

The plan to destroy the bridge was called Operation Squeegee. Two cutters with a paravane strung between them were assigned to sweep within a closely defined off-shore area and destroy the mines as they came to the surface. The *Nootka* kept up a steady bombardment of the shore installations during the sweep and then, once the in-shore areas was clear, moved in closer to shore. Along with the USS *Stickle* the *Nootka* fired on and destroyed some previously unknown marshaling yards, and then turned their attention to destroying the bridge.

After a long bombardment which cut girders, shattered braces, and destroyed the roadway, they expected the bridge to fall. But despite the fact that it was so badly damaged it could never be used again, the Rubber Bridge failed to fall. The *Nootka* eventually sought other targets.

OPERATION SMACK

This ill-conceived and poorly executed operation was described by one journalist, as soldiers dying in a demonstration for the brass. It was in fact a poorly constructed attempt to use an attack on the enemy at Spud Hill, as a training activity and a public relations effort. It was both a military and public relations disaster.

Operation SMACK was an effort by the United States 7th Infantry Division, to test a joint air-tank-artillery-infantry coordinated attack during January, 1953. Several ranking Air Force and Army officers and even some members of the press, were invited to witness the combined effort. The attack was by the 31st Infantry Regiment and the object was to take possession of Spud Hill, just east of T-Bone.

Unfortunately in order for those in attendance to understand what was happening, a rather elaborate six-page brochure was produced which contained the poorly selected word "scenario." Many persons focused on this word and the press had a field day, claiming that it was a show, Hollywood style, for the brass.

While this was not true, the military expended 224,000 pounds of bombs and 220,000 rounds of artillery in the pre-attack, and then just about everything that could go wrong, did. Equipment failed, the air support which was brought in hit the wrong target, leaders became confused. The 7th Division members were halted in a draw and had to turn back. The results of the effort were a failed attack which cost seventy-three lives while claiming only sixty-five of the enemy.

There was a brief congressional investigation in which the facts came out. It was not an exhibition for disinterested spectators but a well intentioned effort to provide critiques and learning from witnessing a joint-attack-effort. No action was taken as the result of the investigation, but the experiment failed

OPERATION TOMAHAWK

People do not usually associate airborne troop drops with the Korean War. The rapid movement, and the difficult topography in Korea, did not lend itself to the airborne speciality. During the Korean War, however, the 187th Airborne Regimental Combat Team (RCT) served in a variety of functions. The 187th ACT arrived at Kimpo Field on September 24, 1950 and took part in the battle for Seoul, the South Korean capital. And, on two occasions, performed in their primary role conducting parachute borne aerial assaults

The first drop was into the Sicken-Sun chon area on October 20, 1951. They were released about thirty miles north of the North Korean capital at Pyongyang. The mission was to cut off the retreating North Korean People's Army and to rescue a group of American POWs that were reported to be dragged along with the retreating troops. The drop resulted in 46 jump casualties, 654 battle casualties, and the capture of 3,818 North Korean prisoners. Unfortunately none of the American POWs sought were found.

The second, and the operation that was called Tomahawk, was launched against Munsan-ni on March 24, 1951. In this effort the airborne unit was supported by the 2nd and 4th Ranger Companies, and was carried over the drop zone in World War II C-46s. The drop involved 3,447 men in an effort to block, and hopefully destroy, the North Korean I Corps. General Ridgway had planned to drop with his troops, as he had in Normandy, but finally settled for observing the attack from an observation plane that followed along. The drop caused 84 injuries, and one was killed and eighteen wounded. The push was able to drive I Corps further north, but were not able to trap them as anticipated.

Operation Tomahawk was not very successful. The drop force was confused by some navigational errors, and unexpected high winds. And there was considerable feeling that the North Koreans had advanced warning of the drop. The 187th Airborne continued to fight in Korea in a variety of situation.

OPERATION TOUCHDOWN

For more than two weeks, beginning in September 1951, the United Nations Command, United States 2nd Infantry Division, advancing on the west of the First Marine Division attempted to take Heartbreak Ridge. When this failed a new plan was constructed. The plan, called Operation Touchdown, was to spread out the North Korean defenders by attacking several adjacent hills at the same time. The specific target was Hill 1220. Mobile support was to be provided by M-4 tanks which arrived on a road prepared by the 2nd Combat Engineers.

The attack was launched on October 5th, with the 23rd Infantry including a French Battalion, and ended on the 15th.

OPERATION YO-YO

The official name of this large scale effort was Operation Tailboard. It was also called "Operation What-in-the-hell." The plan was to move the Tenth Corps from its success at Inchon to the port of Wonsan in order to launch a second amphibious landing. From Inchon it was 850 sea miles to Wonsan. This would create a dual force to close in on the retreating North Korean People's Army. The First Marine Division was put aboard the transports of Task Force 90 and headed for Wonsan, one of the most important strategic positions on the Japanese Sea.

When it was decided to move the 7th Infantry overland to the port of Pusan, and then by sea to Iwon, there were some who asked why the Marines could not go in the same fashion. The load on logistics was almost more than the port of Inchon could handle, and this was greatly aggravated by the demands of time. But no one forced the issue. The invasion force began to collect on

October 4, 1950.

The amphibious aspect of this operation fell on Admiral Struble. The 7th Division left Inchon by rail and road for Pusan where they boarded ships to land at Iwon north of Wonsan. The plan called for an amphibious landing at Wonsan on October 20, 1950. While the East Coast is rugged, the delta of the Namdae River area was acceptable for an amphibious landing. Two days later operational headquarters was moved from the *Mt. McKinley* and opened at Wonsan. Everything went according to plan until the ships arrived in the Wonsan area to discover that the harbor was heavily mined. October 20th came and went as the valiant minesweepers tried to clear the harbor.

In the meantime the transports steamed back and forth in the Sea of Japan just beyond Wonsan. The Transport and Tractor Group arrived and waited. As they waited at sea, the ROK had advanced more quickly than estimated and took the port city. Also, as they waited, dysentery broke out hitting the crews of two cruisers. On board the MSTS transport *Marine Phoenix* more than a third of the troops were affected. Finally, on October 25th the Marines made an administrative landing. Twenty-one transports and fifteen LST came into the harbor and troops began to offload on the 26th at Yellow and Blue beaches. The port was pronounced clear on November 2, 1950.

When they arrived they were greeted by Bob Hope who had brought his USO troupe to entertain the troops. The Marines called it Operation Yo-Yo.

Chapter 8

The United Nations Force

The United Nations! Someone needs to tell me what is united about them?

GI

The Korean War is acknowledged as the first United Nations military action. The number of nations participating in this effort is usually given at twenty-seven, but this figure depends a great deal on how one counts. When the call went out to member nations to come to the aid of South Korea, several countries were quick to respond; about seventeen sent military aid. Some provided troops, others vehicles, some ships and crews, a few sent planes or artillery. Other nations, either unable or unwilling to commit troops, provided materials, bases, transportation, equipment or, as in several cases, medical support. Many made the effort to at least offer some moral support for those involved.

To acknowledge fully the Korean War, it is necessary to understand something about the contributions of the various member nations. By far the majority of troops involved, other than those of the Republic of South Korea, were American. In the main, the UN war in Korea was fought by the armed forces of the United States. Something around 96 percent of the total cost in men and materials was borne by America.

The contribution of member nations was small. A number of nations had limited resources, and their contribution could only be small in comparison to the United States. But the political and psychological impact of United Nations sponsorship, the advantage of fighting under the United Nations flag, was of major significance. Still, while there has been some recognition of the role of the United Nations as an institution, there has been little acknowledgment of the nature and extent of the contributions made by other nations. Interestingly, one of the nations whose role has been minimized is the Republic of South Korea. Despite its lack of economic and political stability, it placed a significant force in the field and fought with desperation for its freedom.

THE REPUBLIC OF SOUTH KOREA

The military force available to Syngman Rhee's new nation was a fifteen-thousand-man Korean Constabulary transformed into the Republic of Korea Army (ROKA) in August 1948. Encouraged and trained by the United States, the ROKA, by 1949 expanded to more than sixty thousand. When the Korean War broke out in June 1950, the military consisted of ninety-eight thousand persons formed into I, II and III Corps, comprising seven undermanned divisions: The First, Second, Third, Fifth, Sixth, Seventh, and the Capital Divisions.

At the center of the military machine was the highly developed 1st Korean Marine Corps Regiment. It was organized in 1949 and had about three thousand men. The unit, briefly attached to the U.S. 5th Marine Regiment during the early part of the war, was involved at the Inchon landing. Following that, for a brief period it was under the control of the ROK Army. Finally, it was attached to the First Marine Division on a permanent basis. In effect, it became a fourth regiment of the division, and it included three infantry battalions and one artillery battalion, and one tank company. The 2^{d} Marine Regiment served as a defensive force to protect the small islands along both coasts.

The Republic of Korea Navy was, at best, small and underdeveloped. At the outbreak of the Korean War it consisted of one frigate, the *Bak Soo San*. The *Bak Soo San* had been purchased from the United States by subscription, by a group of Korean naval officers. The navy also had one LST and fifteen motor minesweepers. As the war went on, however, the United States began to supply the ROKN with ships, and by the end of the war, the Korean navy also included the frigates *Kum Kang San, Apnok, Chi Ri San,* and *Sam Kak San.* The Korean coast guard, which consisted of lightly armed sampans and junks, played a fairly insignificant role.

The ROK Air Force was in even worse shape. Established on October 10, 1951, it consisted of ten T-6 trainers, and thirty-nine trained pilots. By 1953 it had a few F-51 Mustangs. In addition, the ROK had a strong Internal Security Battalion. The armed forces of the Republic of Korea peaked, in July 1953, at 590,011 men and women. Many of these served in KATUSA units. South Korean units reported a total of 225,784 dead.

The ROK Army received a good deal of criticism, especially in the early months, primarily from the military but eventually from the American and British historical community. This criticism eased as the war went on, but there is always the suggestion that ROK troops did not fight well. It is true few of its forces were exceptionally well trained or led. But in the main, the men and women of the armed forces of the Republic of Korea were committed and courageous. In most cases they fought to the fullest degree allowed by their training and equipment. In the beginning particularly, and largely as the result of American policy, they were not trained in unit action, nor did they have heavy weapons. The ROK was simply no match for the experienced, well-equipped, and well-trained NKPA.

Gen. Paik Sun Yup, in his book *From Pusan to Panmunjom* [1992], writes with less than pure objectivity that the ROK was not weak nor its men and women lacking in courage, that what weakness they showed was the result of poor training. The truth lies somewhere in the middle. There is no doubt that they carried a major load, and they suffered most of the casualties.

THE UNITED STATES ARMY

All of America's armed forces saw action in Korea, with the exception of the Coast Guard. The U.S. Army was to be the primary service. The "citizen soldier" would prove once again Gen. Erwin Rommel's view that "American troops knew less but learned faster than any fighting men (I) opposed" [Fehrenbach 1963:3]. The military machine put into Korea to fight the North Korean aggression was primarily American, and as always, the basic load was carried by the foot soldier. There is no doubt the marines, as well as other services, made a serious contributions, but in terms of numbers they were a small part of the American force.

When the United States began to pull its forces out of Korea in accordance with the occupation agreement , it left behind a small military group to serve as an advisory body for the ROKA. It was to serve, as well, as the liaison for the distribution of limited equipment made available. This was the Korean Military Advisory Group (KMAG), established on July 1, 1949. The group consisted of about five hundred men, and was commanded by Brig. Gen, William L. Roberts. Its men were in South Korea as advisors until June 24, 1950.

When the North Koreans crossed the border, the outnumbered and poorly prepared South Korean forces seemed to melt before them, retreating in an effort to find some line it could defend. The KMAG retreated with them. KMAG offered whatever help it could and, on occasion, it added its limited weight to the effort to stop the advancing troops. (Remaining in Korea after the war, they took on the task of providing communication and worked to create better understanding between the ROK and the large number of American troops entering Korea.)

The U.S. forces involved in the war consisted of the Eighth Army in Korea (USEAK), later simply Eighth Army. Eighth Army consisted of corps, one of which at one time served as an independent unit. The designation *corps* has a rather specific meaning: an organizational subunit, composed of two or more divisions, that operates within a field army. A corps is designed for specific battle purposes, and its makeup will change considerably based on the mission assigned to it. A corps is commanded by a major or lieutenant general and usually has few logistical or support units, other than some artillery.

I Corps, arrived in Japan on August 13, 1950, and served as the primary battle corps of Eighth Army. It had no fixed combat structure but its headquarters was the command entity for U.S. and Republic of Korea divisions as well as artillery battalions.

IX Corps was reactivated for the war and arrived in Korea September 23, 1950, when the unit became operational. Primarily a battlefield headquarters, it served with Eighth Army for the remainder of the war.

XVI Corps was established as a headquarters in Japan but did not see action.

X Corps, had a somewhat unusual battle record in Korea. It was called into service around the GHQ Far East Command staff as an independent headquarters for the planning and execution of the invasion of Inchon. After the success of the invasion, and the recapture of Seoul, MacArthur, rather than disband the unit and return it to Eighth Army, sent it east to Wonsan. After the battle at Chosin and the subsequent retreat, most of X Corps withdrew through Hungnam, in December 1950. The corps was returned to Eighth Army control at the insistence of General Ridgway.

Over the course of the war the following were the major units involved in the fighting. Attached, in support, would be numerous transportation, supply, engineering, and independent units serving under a variety of command structures. American divisions were often limited to two infantry regiments.

The Second Infantry Division was composed of the 9th, 23^d, and 38th Infantry Regiments. In support were the 503^d (later the 12th), 15th, 37th, and 38th Artillery Battalions, the 72^d Medium Tank Battalion, the Second Engineering Battalion, and the 82^d Anti-Aircraft Artillery Battalion; and the Second Reconnaissance Company. Organized in October 1917 as the "Indianhead" Division, the Second Division fought in World War I and at Normandy during World War II. It was stationed at Fort Lewis, Washington, in 1950. The Second Division entered Korea in July and was immediately put into the defense of the Naktong perimeter. It was overwhelmed and nearly destroyed by the powerful Communist Chinese forces in the Kunu-ri area. Reconstituted, the division fought at the Punch Bowl, and the Iron Triangle, among other places. During the war it suffered 25,093 casualties. The Second Division returned to Korea in 1965.

The Third Infantry Division was organized in 1917. It fought at Aisne-Marne, where it gained the nickname Third "Marne," and participated in ten campaigns during World War II. It was composed of the 7th, 15th and 30th Infantry Regiments (the 30th was later replaced by the 65th Puerto Rico); the Ninth, Tenth, 39th, and 58th Artillery Battalions, the 64th Tank Battalion, Tenth Engineering Battalion, the Third Reconnaissance Company, and Third AA Battalion.

The Seventh "Hourglass" Infantry Division, sometimes called the "Bayonet Division," included the 17th, 31st, 32^d Infantry Regiments; the 31st, 48th, 49th, and 57th Artillery Battalions, the 73^d Tank Battalion, 13th Combat Engineering Battalion, 15th AA Battalion, and the 7th Reconnaissance Company. The Seventh, organized in December 1917, fought in World War II, and in 1945 it was sent to Korea to disarm the Japanese south of the 38th Parallel. It moved to Hokkaido, Japan, in 1949. Used as replacements when the Korean War first broke out, the Seventh Division, reenforced with KATUSAs, landed at Inchon on September 17, 1950. Later it was transported to the east coast and landed at Iwon, north of Wonsan, with X Corps. It was evacuated, along with others, at Hungnam at Christmas 1950. They were on the central front and the Iron Triangle, and it was at Pork Chop Hill when the armistice was signed. The Seventh Division suffered 15,126 casualties. The division remained in Korea.

The 24th Infantry, nicknamed the "Victory Division," was made up of the 19th, 21st, and 34th Infantry Regiments; the 11th, 13th, 52d, 63d Artillery Battalions, and the 78th Tank Battalion, Third Engineering Battalion, 26th AA Battalion, and 24th Reconnaissance Company. The 24th and its sister division, the 25th, were formed out of the Hawaiian Division, which was split in October 1941. The 24th was at Pearl Harbor when the Japanese attacked and participated in amphibious landings at New Guinea, Leyte, and the southern Philippines. The 24th Division was on occupation duty in Japan when the Korean War broke out. The first to fight in Korea, its 21st Infantry Regiment, called Task Force Smith, was badly decimated in an attempt to delay the enemy. Involved in the push to the Yalu, it was forced to retreat during the Communist Chinese advance. It was later re-formed, minus the 5th Infantry Regiment, into the Fifth Regimental Combat Team. It suffered 11,889 casualties.

The second half of the old Hawaiian Division, was the 25th Infantry Division, and at the time of the war it included the 24th (later the 14th), 27th, and 35th Infantry Regiments; the Eighth, 64th, 69th, 90th Artillery Battalion; and the 79th Tank Battalion, 65th Engineering, 21st AA Battalion, and the 25th Reconnaissance Company. Called the "Tropic Lightning Division" it fought in the Guadalcanal, Solomon, and Luzon campaigns. It was in Japan on occupation duty when the war began. Elements of the division landed in Korea during July 1950 and entered the defense of the Naktong perimeter. It fought with Communist Chinese forces at Chongchon and took part in the battle of the Iron Triangle and at the Reno, Vegas, and Berlin outposts. It suffered 13,685 casualties.

The 40th Infantry Division was a National Guard unit from California. Lieutenant General Ridgway wanted to use the 40th and 45th Infantry Divisions as replacement pools, on an individual basis, but the National Guard demanded, and got, the right to fight as units. The 40th consisted of the 160th, 223d, an 224th Infantry Regiments; the 143d, 625th, 980th, and 981st Field Artillery Battalions, the 14th Tank Battalion, the 40th Reconnaissance Company, and the 578th Engineering Battalion. The "Sunshine Division" was organized in 1917 but was not involved in World War I. The division was reactivated in 1941 and served in the Bismarck Archipelago and in the Phillippines. It arrived in Korea as part of the occupation force to disarm the Japanese and remained until 1946, when it was deactivated. In September it was recalled and reinforced with experienced officers and noncommissioned officers. It replaced the 24th Infantry Division on the front and participated in every campaign after that until the armistice. The division suffered 1,848 casualties.

The 45th Infantry Division was made up of 179th, 180th, and 279th Infantry

Regiments; the 158th, 171st, and 189th Artillery Battalions; and the 245th Tank Battalion, 14th Anti-Aircraft Artillery Battalions, the 45th Reconnaissance Company and 120th Engineering Battalion. The 45th was a National Guard Division from Oklahoma and was known as the "Thunderbird Division." It was called to duty in 1940, operating in the European theater, including Anzio. In 1946 it was deactivated. In December 1951, it replaced the First Cavalry Division on the front in Korea, participating in four campaigns until the armistice in July 1953. The division was released from active duty in 1954. It suffered 4,038 casualties in Korea.

The First Cavalry Division was composed of horse cavalry outfits that had made their reputations against the Indians on America's frontier. During World War II it fought as light infantry in the Pacific. It was the First that entered Manila with Gen. Douglas MacArthur. It had been selected by MacArthur to lead the landing on Japan if that became necessary. Its units were the 5th, 7th, and 8th, Cavalry Regiments; the 61st, 77th, 82[d], and 99th Artillery Battalions; and A Company of the 71th Tank Battalion, 8th Engineering Battalion, 92[d] AA Battalion, and 16th Reconnaissance Company. It landed in Korea on July 18, 1950. It was often referred to as "Gary Owens, from the cavalry song. The 7th Regiment was General MacArthur's color guard. Originally 7,500 short of strength, the division fought hard, but the expectations placed on it were unrealistic.

It was the first unit to confront the Communist Chinese forces, and it fought during the retreat. It was replaced on the line by the 45th Infantry Division and reassigned to Japan where it took on the role of reserve. The First Cavalry Division suffered 16, 498 casualties, more than four times the casualties it took in World War II–not only because of poor deployment but due to infighting among regimental commanders. The First Cavalry would later become the First Airmobile Division.

The Fifth Regimental Combat Team could trace its roots to the War of 1812. In support were the 555th Field Artillery, and a regimental tank unit. This unit served with the 71st Infantry Division during World War II and was deactivated in 1946. Recalled three years later, it was sent to Seoul. It went to Hawaii in 1950 and then back to Korea, July 31, 1950. It first fought independently, then with the 24th Infantry Division; from January 1952 until the armistice it operated independently under IX and X Corps. It suffered 4,422 casualties. The 29th Regimental Combat Team was committed to combat on July 25, 1950, near the Naktong River line. Located on Okinawa it only had two of the authorized three battalion. Both battalions were eventually integrated into the 25th Infantry Division.

The well-known 187th Airborne Regimental Combat Team was also in Korea. This force started as a glider unit, but by 1950 it was a parachute force of about four thousand men, supported by the 674th Field Artillery Battalion. The 187th RCT arrived at Kimpo airfield on September 26 and joined the battle for Seoul. The "Rakkasans" made two airborne assaults. It also fought on several occasions as conventional infantry. Originally a part of the 11th Airborne Division, it became independent in February 1951. During the Korean War it suffered 2,115 casualties, 442 of them killed.

The war in Korea was fought by "retreads"–those called back into active service after being discharged at the end of World War II–and by reservists and draftees who had been caught despite a highly refined system of deferments. The draft in effect at the time of the Korean War provides some insight into national priorities. The first modern draft, in anticipation of World War II, was on September 16, 1940. It allowed college students to complete their school year and gave postponements to men in actual war jobs or in training for them. By June 1943, only medical and veterinary school students were deferred. On March 31, 1947, conscription came to an end. Conscription was considered in 1948 and then reestablished abruptly in June 1950. At that point, U.S. forces numbered less than 600,000; 650,000 reservists and National Guard troops needed to be recalled to active duty. As the draft expanded, several special-interest groups called for deferments.

The segment of young males in college was briefly protected, but on May 26, 1951, all students were required to take the Selection Service College Qualification Test (SCAD). The test was graded by a committee of university faculty from Harvard, and the universities of Columbia, Illinois and Iowa. The Selective Service set a minimum of 70 percent in order to be deferred for college attendance. Obviously it was impossible to flunk the test, but those who did not reach a minimum score were destined for the draft. About 63 percent of those who took the test did not meet the standards expected. Another 15 percent did not reach the minimum score but received an automatic deferment because of their high class standing.

By January 1952 the deferment system was protecting three students for every industrial worker who was deferred. In the scheme, fathers were also exempt. Interestingly, while undergraduates were fairly safe, graduate students and research assistants were not. Of those men eligible for the draft, about 25 percent eventually avoided service: two-thirds were found to be unfit for combat, and one-third were deferred for other reasons. The figures were approximately 909,000 who were excused for dependency, 110,000 because of significant occupations, and more than 850,000 as students.

There had been many changes in the draft and troop placement system after World War II. The changes had many unexpected and negative results. Unlike World War I, where men were drafted by geographical area, and unlike the system in World War II, where troop replacement was primarily by units, the Korean War system called, replaced, and rotated soldiers on an individual basis. As discussed above, a point system was used for rotation from the line; the closer the soldier was to combat, the more points he received. As noted, a significant outcome was a decline in unit identification, organizational pride, and even combat efficiency.

This poor efficiency was the result of what would later be called "the empty battlefield syndrome"–that is a lack of people in the field of battle to whom the individual soldier relates. It has long been understood that many soldiers do not fight because of patriotism, or lofty ideas, but for those who are with them–their "buddies." With decreased unit identification there was a corresponding decrease in battlefield loyalty.

THE UNITED STATES NAVY

Korea is very much an island, though surrounded only on three sides by water. Its geography meant that the U.S. Navy would be heavily involved. In fact, the importance of the navy in the war is hard to overstate. Yet the historical accounting of the Korean War has tended to overlook its role. For years there were only two basic works on the navy in the Korean War, Malcolm Cagle's and Frank Manson's *The Sea War in Korea* [1957] and James Field's *History of the United States Naval Operations: Korea* [1962]. Both works are excellent but now totally outdated. Recently some good new materials have become available about particular aspects of the navy role. These works range from studies of carrier operations to recollections of life aboard an escort destroyer.

When the war broke out, the U.S. naval force available in Korean waters consisted of four destroyers (the USS *Mansfield, DeHaven, Collett, Lyman K. Swenson)* and the cruiser USS *Juneau.* The *Juneau* delivered the first major punch on June 28, 1950, when it fired on positions near Samchok. Command was exercised by Naval Forces Far East (NAVFE), which provided headquarters services and had command control over the Seventh Fleet and British Commonwealth naval forces.

The United Nations naval presence consisted of several task forces. The essential units were Task Force 77, the fast carrier force; Task Force 90, the amphibious force, and Task Force 95, the blockading, logistic, and escort force. Its commander was first Vice Admiral C. Turner Joy and then Vice Admiral Robert P. Briscoe.

During the war several aircraft carriers served operational tours: The USS *Valley Forge, Bon Homme Richard, Antietam, Boxer, Lake Champlain, Kearsarge, Philippine Sea, Oriskany, Leyte, Essex,* and the *Princeton.* The blockading and escort force was accompanied by the light carrier the USS *Bataan* and four escort carriers, USS *Badoeng Strait, Biroke, Rendova,* and *Sicily.* Several battleships were brought back into service the USS *Iowa, Missouri, Wisconsin,* and the *New Jersey.* In mid-September 1950, the navy under, Admiral Struble, carried out the tremendous job of the amphibious landing at Inchon. In a pre-invasion bombardment, destroyers and cruisers first softened up Wolmi-do, the harbor island, and then turned on the enemy troops at Inchon. On September 15, marines from the First Marine Division landed successfully. Their transportation, support, and protection were provided by a fleet of 261 ships, representing seven nations.

Less than a month later, the navy took the troops and the equipment of X

Corps to the opposite coast, landing them at Wonsan and Iwon. Two months later the navy was involved in the largest evacuation America had ever experienced. Retreating before massive Communists Chinese forces, the UN troops were met at Hungnam where on December 24, 1950, the navy completed the evacuation of nearly a hundred thousand troops and about that many civilian refugees. Similar, though less massive, evacuations were occurring all along both coasts, while naval forces held back the Communists.

The navy provided 1,842,000 personnel during the war. Of these, 458 officers and men were killed in action, 5,979 were injured or wounded. The degree of the naval involvement can perhaps be more easily seen in the fact that it fired more than four million rounds of ammunition, and damaged 3,334 buildings and 824 vessels, as well as numerous trucks, railway locomotives, tanks, bridges, and supply dumps. In addition, it accounted for an estimated 28,566 casualties among the enemy.

One of the more interesting episodes was the United Nations blockade and bombardment of Wonsan. This siege was the longest sustained naval blockade in American naval history. Over more than two years of continuous surface and air attacks, Wonsan had suffered heavy damage. Port facilities and transportation centers were hit by destroyers, cruisers, attack planes, and even the 16-inch guns of the battleships. It is estimated that the North Koreans kept more than thirty thousand troops in the Wonsan area to guard the beach against a potential landing. North Korean artillery located in the hills was able to return fire, even hitting some of the United Nations ships.

NAVFE was also responsible for the Military Sea Transportation Service (MSTS), which provided the sea lift of men and materials to the front. It was nearly five thousand nautical miles from the United States to Japan, and on to Korea. More than one hundred ships served in the support force, which supplied whatever was needed, replenishing combatant ships as close to their assigned areas as possible, and providing fuel, ammunition and food.

A major factor in the Korean War was the "little" ship. Among these, the minesweepers were to play a highly significant role. It was on the smaller ships that the danger was the greatest. At Wonsan harbor for example, of every twenty-five minesweepers, one was lost. Landing ships of numerous varieties, were gathered up from every available source to provide transportation, move goods and supplies, and land deliver men and equipment during the assaults. These sturdy vessels were used as well for ship-to-ship communications, reconnaissance, and patrol. Many of these ships were in the amphibious forces and supported naval beach groups and underwater demolition teams.

Both sea based and land based patrol squadrons kept the fleet abreast of enemy activity, functioned as a rescue service, and supported the Formosa force assigned to keep the Nationalists' stronghold free from conflict.

Task Force 77 launched its first planes from the *Valley Forge* against the North Korean capital of Pyongyang. The *Valley Forge*'s July 3, 1950, launch was not only the first naval air strike against the North Korean enemy, but the first time that American jets had been used in combat. Throughout the war, naval planes were used in air operations of all kinds—interdiction, strike, ground support, and bombing missions against air fields, plants, factories, railroads, tunnels, supply areas, and fuel dumps. They also provided air cover for the fleet. They were involved in some air-to-air combat, but in the main, the planes of the Communist countries stayed away from the ships.

The U.S. Navy air, which included the Marine aviation, flew approximately 276,000 sorties, dropped nearly 179,000 tons of bombs, and fired more than 71 million rounds of ammunition.

THE UNITED STATES MARINES

The Marine Corps units in Korea consisted primarily of the First Marine Division and the First Marine Aircraft Wing, with some support services. Cut by postwar releases and stringent budget controls, the Corps consisted of only 73,279 men and women when it was called upon for Korea. When General MacArthur requested the First Marine Division for his Inchon landing, it was necessary to rebuild it. In July 1950, thirty-three thousand reservists were called up. As the rest of the division was forming, the marines command put together the First Marine Brigade, under Brig. Gen. Edward A. Craig. The First Brigade landed in Pusan, and it joined with the 25th Infantry Division (Army) before being pulled out for the Inchon invasion. The First Marine Division included 1st, 5th, and 7th, Marine Regiments; the 1st, 2d, 3d, and 4th Battalions; the 11th Artillery Regiment; and the 1st Tank Battalion; 1st Engineering Battalion, and 1st Amphibious Battalion. The 7th Regiment came later, joining the division after Inchon. The Marines supplied their own air support, including observation aircraft and the newly introduced helicopters.

The First Marine Aircraft Wing began its Korean operations in September 1950, with Corsairs and Tigercats flown from shore. Later it added Skyraiders, Panther jets, Banshees, and the F3D Skyknight fighter.

THE UNITED STATES AIR FORCE

In many respects, this was the first war for the U.S. Air Force. Having fought in World War II as the Army Air Corps, then the Army Air Force, it finally became the U.S. Air Force in 1947. The war in Korea was not the sort of war the air force, or the Joint Chiefs of Staff, had expected to fight, but it responded to the demand. The Far East Air Force was organized as a component of General MacArthur's command. It consisted of the Fifth Air Force, as the primary unit, and the 13th Air Force, the 20th Air Force, and tactical wings.

FEAF bomber commands employed B-29 Superfortresses, heavy bombers that were used in a wide variety of missions against bridges, tunnels, railway centers, factories, troop centers, airfields, dams, manufacturing centers, and supply routes. One of the more significant roles they undertook was the neutralization of more than a dozen enemy tactical airfields in North Korea.

While the Korean War produced a great deal of controversy about the effectiveness of air-ground support, most would agree FEAF aircraft were essential. It may not have been an "air war," as some like to suggest. However, on some occasions the air component was highly necessary–for example to screen United Nations troops that were forced into the Pusan perimeter in September 1950.

Combat cargo operations were essential, especially early in the war. The 374th Troop Carrier Wing, equipped with C-54 four-engine transports, was about all that was available when the war broke out. Its first official use was to evacuate personnel from Korea. The 21st Troop Carrier, which used C-47s, was responsible for flying units of the 24th Infantry Division into the conflict. Considering the poor conditions, transport operations were often a test of the skill of the pilots. Under the command of Maj. William H. Turner, who had organized both "the Hump" and the Berlin airlift, the Combat Cargo Command was developed. It included the 374th, the 21st and 1st troop carrier units, and the 314th Troop Carrier Wing. On January 25, 1951, the provisional command became 315th Air Wing. From that point on, many of the methods worked out, and air cargo operations, became more routine.

The Combat Cargo Command, the 315th Air Wing, flew C-46s, C-47s, C-54s, C-119 Flying Boxcars, and C-124 Globemasters. They moved significant amounts of supplies–medicine, blood, vaccine, radar, and mail, among other things–and personnel into Korea and they flew UN wounded from Korea to Japan. In addition they airlifted in excess of 1,500 airborne troops on one occasion, using more than a hundred aircraft and 160 round trips.

THE UNITED KINGDOM

The contribution of Great Britain was of major significance and should not be underestimated. This is true as well for those nations identified within the Commonwealth– Australia, Canada and New Zealand. The British people had suffered greatly during World War II and were hardly back to normal before they were called upon to go to war again. The decision to come to the aid of South Korea, and thus, in the larger sense, of the United States and the United Nations, was difficult and complex. The story of the Commonwealth contribution is well related in Jeffery Grey's short but insightful account, *The Commonwealth Armies and the Korean War: An Alliance Study* [1988]. But the political, and well as the military, maneuvering of the British government is worth an advanced study of its own.

The United Kingdom responded almost immediately with ships. The ships that saw service included the carriers HMS *Theseus, Glory, Ocean,* and *Triumph,* and the cruisers HMS *Kenya, Ceylon, Belfast, Jamaica, Birmingham,* and *Newcastle.* In support the British provided the destroyers HMS *Charity, Cossack, Consort, Cockade,* and *Comus;* and the frigates *Black Swan, Alarcity, Heart, Morecombie Bay, Whitesands Bay,* and the hospital ship *Maine.*

While the Commonwealth units were often large enough to be employed independently in tactical situations, the British often fought with, and frequently under the command of, American forces. The first ground force to arrive was an advanced group of the British Commonwealth 27th Brigade. It went into action almost immediately along the Naktong River. It was soon followed by the British 29th Infantry Brigade.

By July 1951, all units of the British Commonwealth Forces were formed into the First Commonwealth Division. Because the British, as well as the Commonwealth nations, rotated their troops by unit rather than individually, several different units were involved. These would include, for the British, battalions of the Middlesex, Argyll, and Sutherland Highlanders, King's Shropshire Light Infantry, King's Own Scottish Borderers, Durham Light Infantry, Royal Fusiliers, Royal Nurthumberland Fusilers, Glosters, Royal Ulster Rifles, Royal Leicesters, Welch Regiment, Royal Norfolk, Black Watch, Duke of Wellington's, King's (Liverpool) Regiments; for the Australians battalions of the Royal Australian Regiment,; for the Canadians battalions of the Princess Patricia's Canadian Light Infantry, Royal Canadian Regiment, Royale 22th Regiment.

The armored units consisted of segments from the King's Royal Irish Hussars, the 1st, 5th, and 7th Royal Tank Regiments, the Royal Inniskilling Dragoon Guards, and Lord Strathcona's Horse. Artillery was from the 45th, 14th, 120th, 42d, 20th, 16th Field Regiment (NZ), Royal Artillery, Independent Light, Independent Mortar, Royal New Zealand, Royal Canadian Horse, and Royal Canadian artillery units.

In support of Commonwealth troops were the 55th Royal Engineers, the 57th Canadian Independent Field Squadron, the 28th Field Engineer Regiment, and the 64th Field Park Squadron. The medical units were the 60th Indian Field Ambulance, 26th, 25th, 37th, and 38st Field Ambulance, Royal Army Medical Corps, and the 25th Canadian Field Dressing Station. The first ground force to arrive in support of the United States was an advanced group of the British Commonwealth 27th Brigade. It went into action along the Naktong River on 29 August 1950. In November the United Kingdom Brigade aided in the retreat from Seoul, joining in the January 1951 counterattack. The contingent supplied by the Commonwealth included several air units, in addition to carrier planes. In June 1950, Royal Australian Air Force provided one RAAF squadron and an air communications unit. These squadrons flew F-51 Mustangs until the 77th Squadron started flying Mentor-8 jets.

For political reasons, Canada decided to form a special unit to fulfill what it considered its responsibility to aid the United Nations. This new unit of, 7,065 was to be drawn primarily as volunteers from somewhere other than the regular army. It was formed as the 25th Infantry Brigade and placed under the command of Brigadier J. M. Rockingham. The brigade was in action by the beginning of 1951. It consisted of three battalions of infantry and one regiment of artillery, as well as a field ambulance unit.

SMALLER NATIONS

Norway was involved nearly from the beginning. The Norwegian Red Cross was made available first. After November 1951, the Norwegian army supplied a mobile army surgical hospital, called "Normash." The 106 medical personnel assigned were in the country from mid-November of 1951 until January 1955. Norway also supplied merchant ships of small tonnage.

Shortly after the invasion at Inchon, a battalion combat team of the Philippine Expeditionary Force joined with the United Nations forces. Its 1,367 soldiers were formed into three rifle companies, a reconnaissance light tank company, a self-propelled artillery battery, and support services. They arrived at Pusan in September 1950 and operated with the 25th Infantry Division, specializing in antiguerrilla activities. Later, they were relieved by the 20th Regimental Combat Team and thereafter by the 19th, the 14th, and 2nd RCTs. The Philippines also made available fifty thousand cakes of soap.

Arriving at Pusan, the First Turkish Brigade, reinforced by the 241st Infantry Regiment, joined with 25th Infantry Division for the advance into North Korea. The unit included artillery, signals, engineers, transport, ordnance and medical units. The Turks fought at Sinnimini, near Osan and in May 1952 they halted a significant Chinese assault. From September 1951 to May 1954 they were replaced in turn by the Second, Third, and Fourth Brigades.

Under the command of Brig. Gen. Tahsin Yazici, the 5,190-member Turkish Infantry Brigade arrived October 12–17, 1950. They were first attached to the 25th Infantry but transferred to IX Corps, later to the Second Infantry Division. The Turks' contribution was controversial, though the U.S. troops spoke highly of the fighting ability. Referred to by many as the "terrible Turks," they were known for their use of the bayonet. A total of 14,936 Turks served; of these 741, died and 2,068 were wounded. The Turkish military did not award medals for valor, but many Turkish soldiers received American decorations.

Thailand provided two corvettes, HTMS *Prasae* and *Bangpakon*; the latter ran aground and was destroyed. It also provided the *Sichang*, a transport for use by its own troops. In October the Royal Thai forces arrived. They consisted of the naval unit above, an air unit, and the 21st Infantry Regiment (later renamed HM Queen Sirikit's Guard Unit). They were attached to the U.S. 24th Infantry Division, then the 187th Regimental Combat Team, which was advancing on Pyongyang, and later the First Cavalry Division. These troops saw action in the 1951 spring offensive and at Port Chop Hill. The regiment departed in 1955 leaving behind a company that served into 1972. Its casualties amounted to 125.

In September 1950, the First South African (Union of South Africa) Air Force sent F-51s of the 2d South African Air Force Squadron, which later flew F-86 jets. It provided all its own necessary ground personnel.

OTHER UNITED NATIONS MEMBERS

Many nations offered support to the United Nations cause. Several nations offered ground troops to fight in Korea. Four nations did not, in the end, send the troops they had promised. The largest contingent of ground forces offered, three infantry divisions of highly seasoned troops, was refused: Truman saw this contingent, offered by Nationalist Chinese general Chiang Kai-shek, as too controversial. Refused as well–the proper terminology was "acceptance deferred"–were thirty officers from Bolivia, volunteers from Costa Rica, El Salvador, and from Panama, and twenty C-47 transports from Nationalist China. At the height of the troop strength, in 1952, approximately thirty-five thousand ground forces provided by United Nations members, and 5,400 air personnel.

With the exception of the British Commonwealth forces and the Turkish troops, the contributions of most nations were of battalion size or less, and so were not available for deployment as independent units. Most were attached to regiments of the U.S. Army, or, on one or two occasions, as regiments attached to divisions.

Not all were effective. The Filipino battalion was not well prepared, and it was not used in combat when that could be avoided. Somewhat the same problem existed with the Thais and Ethiopians. But despite these minor problems, and the fact that all efforts were greatly compounded by the difficulties of language, the integration of units worked fairly well. The contribution of many of these fighting men was larger than the numbers would indicate. All had problems of equipment differences and resupply, which made reinforcement difficult. The different nationalities were of course used to their own methods, and they had trained under vastly different systems, and to fight under different conditions

At the end of the first year, in July of 1951, 6.3 percent of the total force opposed to the North Koreans and Communists Chinese were from member nations other than the United States. The U.S. contribution was 70.4 percent and the ROK 23.3 percent. The remaining 6 percent was made up of many other nations.

The Australians air support was the first to arrive, the Royal Australian Air Force, 77th Squadron, which was equipped with propeller- driven P-51s. They had been stationed in Japan. The P-51s were later replaced with the British Meteor 8. The Australians also provided the 30th Communications Flight and 36th Transport Squadrons, flying C-47 Dakotas, which were united in the 91st Composite Wing. Naval forces included the frigate HMAS *Shoalhaven* and the destroyer HMAS *Bataan*. They joined the British Commonwealth naval force. Later in the war, HMAS *Warramunga* replaced *Shoalhaven*. In October 1951 the Australian navy supplied the carrier HMAS *Sydney*, with the 20th Carrier Air Group. The Australian air group consisted of two propeller-driven squadrons.

A week after the 77th Squadron arrived, the 3d Battalion, Royal Australian Regiment, landed and was attached to the 27th British Commonwealth Brigade. The 1st Battalion arrived in April 1952 and replacement by units continued after that. Before the armistice 1,584 Australians had been wounded, 339 killed, and 29 taken prisoner. The Australians also provided penicillin and, on November 28, 116,000 pounds of laundry soap.

On January 13, 1951, the 1st Belgian Battalion, including Walloon and Flemish companies arrived at Pusan. Its Luxemburg Detachment consisted of forty-eight men, who made up the bulk of the first platoon of Company A. It fought in support of the British 29th Brigade at Imjin, where it made a significant contribution. During the rest of the Korean War, this unit served with the U.S. Third Infantry Division, and it made important stands at Haktang-ni and Chatkil. This nation lost 103 dead. It provided air transport and four hundred tons of sugar

The Royal Canadian Air Force, attached to the U.S. Fifth Air Force, provided twenty pilots and technical officers. Canadian Air Transport Command also served in Korea, and delivering more than thirteen thousand passenger and nearly seven million pounds of freight. Canada also provided some dry-goods vessels, of ten thousand tons or less. The Canadian government provided several naval vessels, all of which saw action; they included the destroyers *Nootka, Haida, Huron, Iroquois, Cayuga, Athabaskan, Sioux,* and *Crusader.* These accounted for eight of the eleven ships in the Canadian destroyer fleet. During the war, 310 officers and men were killed in combat. Another1,202 suffered wounds.

The Colombian frigate *Almirante Padilla* arrived for service in Korean waters in 1950. The 1st Colombian Battalion, the only Latin American ground unit ever to fight in Asia, arrived in Korea in June 1951. This 1,060-man force brought with it a nine-piece band. The battalion joined the United States 24th Infantry Division and took part in the defense of Kumsong. The Colombian unit was later transferred to the Seventh Infantry Division and supported it in the battles of T-Bone Hill and Old Baldy. One hundred and thirty-four members of this contingent were killed in action.

From Denmark the United Nations received medical support, primarily in the form of the hospital ship *Jutlandia,* which was anchored in Pusan harbor and functioned there. Later it was stationed at Inchon. Denmark also provided the motor ship *Bella Dan.* The ships supplied about one hundred medical people, and they remained in Korea until 16 August 1957.

The 1st Kagnew Battalion from Ethiopia was formed from members of Emperor Haile Selassie's imperial guard. This elite group was named after King Menelik's horse in the Ethiopian-Italian War. It also joined with the U.S. Seventh Infantry Division when it arrived in May 1951. The Kagnew fought along the Kansas Line, and later at Sam-Hyon and Tokan-ni. It was on Pork Chop Hill when the armistice was signed. Ethiopian troops remained in Korea until 1967.

Despite their own heavy involvement in the expanding war in Indochina (Vietnam), the French were able to offer some support to the United Nations effort. They made available the frigate *La Grandiere* and also a battalion, including an assault platoon. Arriving through the port of Pusan in late November 1950, the independent Premier Battalion Francais de 1 O.N.U. (also known as Battalions Boeuf and Coree) joined with the U.S. Second Infantry Division. The French fought with great courage at Wonju and in the defense of Chipyong-ni in February 1951, which halted the Chinese offensive. The French troops were also involved at the Punchbowl, Heartbreak Ridge, and Arrow Head Hill. In late October 1953 the French pulled out in favor of their own decisive war, leaving 261 dead in the Korean struggle. French troops won three U.S. Presidential Unit Citations. They were known for their advocacy of the bayonet charge.

On December 9, 1950, a reinforced battalion of volunteers from the Greek army arrived in Korea. The Royal Hellenic Air Force had already supplied the 13th Transport Flight to aid in the massive evacuation of X Corps from Hungnam. The volunteer battalion consisted of 849 men, in three rifle companies. It was assigned to the U.S. First Cavalry Division. The Greek volunteers took part in the capture of Hill 402, Scotch Hill, and Harry Hill, and they served as security guards at the Koje-do prisoner of war camp. The Greek contingent remained in Korea for three years, finally leaving in 1955, having lost 182. The Greeks also supplied eight Dakota transport planes, medical supplies, and soap.

India was very involved in the political maneuvering that went on between the United States, China, and the Soviet Union. While It backed the United Nations decision for involvement in South Korea, it was reluctant to commit its forces. The Indians believed that the Korean War was primarily a confrontation between the United States and Russia, one they did not want to get caught in. However, they were willing to provide aid in the form of the 60th Field Ambulance and Surgical Unit, which served in support of the 27th (later the 28th) British Commonwealth Brigade. The unit included 346 men and seventeen officers. It arrived on November 20, 1950. The later role of India in the exchange of prisoners, and in maintaining the conditions of the armistice, has not been well researched, but was an important role.

The Netherlands provided ground troops consisting of an understrength infantry battalion of some 636 personnel, including some nurses. The unit was filled with volunteers from a wide pool and it was a rather eclectic force. Known as the Dutch Battalion, the full battalion arrived at Pusan on November 23, 1950. It was associated with the U.S. 38th Infantry Regiment (also called the 38th RCT), Second Infantry Division. The Dutch contribution, which included the suppression of prisoners during the riots at Koje-do, was made at the cost of 120 lives. Its naval contribution was the destroyer HNMS *Evertsen,* which joined with the Blockading and Escort Force.

New Zealand sent two frigates, HMNZ *Tutira* and *Pukaki,* which operated with the Blockade and Escort Force. In addition the 16th New Zealand Field Artillery served in Korea, attached to the British Commonwealth Brigade, later the First British Commonwealth Division. The people of New Zealand also provided peas, milk, and two hundred tons of soap.

OTHER AREAS OF SUPPORT

A considerable number of other nations contributed to the war effort without sending troops. Argentina provided canned goods and frozen meat for the United Nations troops stationed in Korea. Brazil offered money. Chile provided strategic materials; Cuba offered sugar, alcohol, and blood. Ecuador provided medical supplies and rice. Iceland, in support of the United Nations cause, provided 125 tons of cod liver oil, and the new state of Israel provided medical supplies. Lebanon sent money, Liberia provided rubber. Mexico sent beans, Panama provided the use of merchant marine vessels, Nicaragua offered rice and alcohol. Pakistan gave wheat; Paraguay sent medical supplies; Peru sent one million shoe soles; Uruguay provided money and blood; and Venezuela sent medical supplies, blankets, and blood.

OTHER INVOLVED NATIONS

It is difficult to understand fully the role played by Japan. When the war began it was an occupied nation, less than five years from defeat. Yet this island nation had a significant part in the United Nations effort in Korea. One of the side issues of the Korean War was the peace treaty with Japan. The Communists were disturbed by the use of Japan, but despite their protest, many Japanese nationals were involved in the war effort. Japan provided as many as forty-six vessels, many of them old U.S. LSTs, and more than 1,200 former Imperial Japanese Navy personnel. Many Japanese sailors served in the combat minesweeping operations in the Korean harbors of Wonsan, Kunson, Inchon, Haeju, and Chinnampo.

Sweden provided the first medical team that arrived. This unit, the Swedish Red Cross, arrived at Pusan on the 23d of September 1950. The Swedes continued to operate a field hospital until April 1957. The Italians, who were also not members of the United Nations, nevertheless allowed their Red Cross to build and run a hospital unit at Yongdungpo.

PARTISANS

Many partisans were finally organized into a unit called the United Nations Partisan Infantry (UNPIK). At the height of the war, in 1953, the unit reached a strength of about twenty-two thousand. There is not much written about the partisan groups, who gave so much, or about the extent of their involvement in the United Nations effort. Fortunately, recently two good books have come out: William Breuer's *Shadow Warriors* [1996] which addresses the covert war, and Ben Malcom's *White Tigers: My Secret War in North Korean* [Brassey 1996]. The groups were mainly North Koreans who volunteered for whatever reason to work under United Nations military forces. The military provided the food, clothes, shelter, and training; in return the partisans conducted raids against North Korean and Communist Chinese lines of communication and supply. Using a fleet of decrepit fishing boats, they raided along the west coasts, aided by American and British soldiers. It was from UNPIK that the U.S. special forces unit known as the Green Berets emerged.

While they had significant success in some of the operations, their contribution to the overall outcome of the war was probably minor. They took part in twenty-two parachute operations, not totally successful. In many cases the lack of success might well be attributed to the immense size of the job they had been given. They received little United Nations support, yet the partisans were expected to wreak havoc on North Korean and Chinese supply and manpower reserves. It was just too big a job.

Chapter 9

Revising the Revisionists

Those who are inclined to blame their enemies may be the smaller heroes,
whose words merely replace bullets to "replay"the old hostility.

Philip West

One historian has described the writing of history as riding in the back of a
pickup being driven rapidly down a very busy street, trying to describe the
situation and events in the previous block. The driver of the car is the leader,
who, in theory, knows where the truck is headed. Ideally this person is a
visionary, at least a politician. In the passenger seat is the journalist, trying to
write down what he or she sees pass quickly by the truck window. Sitting in
the back of the truck, facing the traveled road, is the historian, who is trying
to describe where they have been without knowing where they are going. The
problem is made more difficult because what they are currently leaving behind
is much clearer in the historian's mind than what they left behind only
moments before that. That is, memory, and thus narrative, is greatly affected
by more current impressions.

To complicate the situation, historians are not satisfied with attempts to
record and interpret the past; they must also trace the history of their
historical efforts. Going back to the illustration, they not only record what they
have seen but record the records of what they have recorded. This is not just
preoccupation with themselves; rather, historians seek to know the truth as
clearly as possible by understanding their own discipline. *Historiography,* the
history of histories, is an odd but essential aspect of the historical endeavor.
Written history, like most things, has its fashion and fads, visions and
revisions.

History is written as an unfolding process. Researchers publish the results
of their studies. These results are, in turn, studied and criticized by other
researchers. Critics produce what they see as new and improved works, which
are in turn criticized and expanded upon by other researchers. This process,
as defined by George F. Hegel, is called the *dialectic*: a triad composed of a
thesis, antithesis, synthesis. The thesis and antithesis are in conflict and push

toward a synthesis. The synthesis emerges from, but is different than, either the thesis or anthesis. The synthesis, in turn, becomes the thesis of a new dialectic, and so on. Hegel's ultimate synthesis is "history," but for many historians there is no end to the process.

The writing of Korean War history has moved along in basically the same fashion. The interesting thing is that while the Korean War has not produced the quantity of historical narrative and analysis that one might expect, it has gone through most of the phases of historical writing. However, at the moment–and we are still way too close to it all–the process seems to have moved in leaps and gaps, rather than with the gradual flow so often seen in historical understanding. This has allowed for the acceptance of radical departures from the norm. The analysis moves like a rapidly advancing army. It leaves behind pockets of resistance which in time will need to be addressed more directly.

The written history produced to date reflects a movement through some predictable stages, from the orthodox to a postrevisionist synthesis, though there have been only limited examples of some approaches. There should be no effort to draw too fine a line between the schools of response. The various periods and interpretations have been given names, to make it easy to talk about them; however, the various interpretations are not always easy to identify, and few persons involved can be labeled with historiographical terms without being done some disservice. There is, as well, a wide variety of disagreements within the camps themselves. As in every human endeavor, some points of view appear to be quite extreme. Sometimes they are just bad history. But most have been produced by scholars of ability and integrity.

The term "orthodoxist"is used of historians who report the commonly accepted, customary, and traditional. Interestingly, the paradoxical term "neo-orthodox" has been used to mean those both who are still orthodox as well as former revisionists who have returned to an orthodox point of view. In historical interpretation, "orthodox" often refers to interpretations that support the views of the author's nationality or his or her ideological commitment.

Some narrative histories of the Korean War were published by the end of 1951. Obviously these could not reflect the whole story. A few "histories" written in 1951, reflected the mistaken belief that the Korean War was over. They tended to be very supportive of the positions and policies voiced by the U. S. government. Like Robert Leckie's *Conflict: The History of the Korean War* [Leckie, Robert 1996], they reflect an admiration for the American soldier and support for Washington's conduct of the war. This view is often overly romanticized, but it has dominated the initial studies done in the West. The first historians have tended to reflect the orthodox view.

Several of the studies that came out in the decade following the Korean War heralded the American effort in Korea as having some of the qualities of a "good war," one fought for precise and understandable reasons. The view was fairly simple: the Communists had invaded a democratic and freedom-loving nation, and the United States had stepped in to support the United Nations in repelling the attack. One of the earlier Cold War studies from the orthodox perspective is Herbert Feis, *From Trust to Terror: The Onset of the Cold War, 1945 -1950* [Feis, Herbert 1970]. These views are opposed by what Lester H. Brune calls the "realistic critics," whose works include the theologian Reinhold Niebuhr's *The Irony of American History* [Niebuhr, Reinhold 1952] and statesman George Kennan's *Memoirs* [Kennan, George 1972].

Sometimes the orthodox interpretations are called the "heroic period." This term is used because their authors tend to concentrate on the value of their friends and allies and on the utter and total evil of the enemy. Such views represent a time when historians, like politicians, were still trying to develop a narrative to explain, and justify, the national behavior. Their works are heavily laden with the first blush of military success and the small victories of national pride. Military and political leaders are applauded with biographies so bad they really fall under the genre of campaign biographies. Yet even in the most committed of these works, the moral affirmations and patriotic justifications that had dominated early World War II histories often appeared out of place.

It is important to note that some early historians took a highly critical view of the Korean War. The most important was the popular liberal journalist I. F. Stone. His book, *The Hidden History of the Korean War* [Stone, I. F. 1952], published even before the war was over, was highly critical of America's involvement. Other works critical at an early period would include Melvin B. Voorhees' *Korean Tales* [Voorhees, Melvin 1952] and, as a military counterpoint, T. R. Fehrenbach's classic *This Kind of War* [Fehrenbach, T.R. 103].

During the Vietnam War era, the passionate feelings of the times sparked a new interest in American wars, and in America at war. One response was a rekindling of interest in the Korean War. The result was thinking, and rethinking, about governmental policies and heroic interpretations. These historians "revisited" the earlier view of the Korean experience as a necessary war fought for noble purposes, and they questioned its interpretations. While it is safe to say that the Korean War experience was primarily responsible for triggering the transition of American thought about war, it was not until the 1970s and 1980s that the changing views began to affect the writing of history. The process, however, was to take history from the highly romanticized memory of World War II to the structurally critical response unleashed during the war in Vietnam.

The second stage in the historical process is usually called "revisionism," reflecting new and expanded research into previously unacknowledged material. But it also represents skepticism about earlier interpretations. The revisionist phase features a growing concern with the causes and origins of the war and it shows a more concentrated willingness to challenge the pronouncements of official histories. Korean War revisionists are especially critical of the United States, sensing a confusion of policies as well as hazy and undefined goals. They point to a less than full commitment of energy and resources. They have also been willing to look with greater appreciation at those identified as America's enemies. As a rule they are also very critical of the whole negotiation procedure and the armistice that was signed.

Revisionist would include Gabriel and Joyce Kolko's *The Limits of Power: The World and the United States Foreign Policy, 1945 -1954* [1972]. These reflect a negative interpretation of the pressure, economic and military, that America was putting on the Soviet Union. One of the more acceptable revisionist pieces on the Cold War is William LaFeber's *America, Russia and the Cold War 1945-1975* [1967]. Much of the revisionists' argument is that Washington misunderstood China and thus made major mistakes.

This American miscalculation went so far as to produce an economic expansion that was frightening to the Soviet Union. This is well stated in Steven I. Levine's "Soviet-American Rivalry in Manchuria and the Cold War" [1977]. Not all revisionist's work is well accepted. Warren Goldstein, in "Bad History Is Bad Culture," observes that revisionists are "pedantic, humorless, 'scholar-squirrels'." He goes on to quote Gore Vidal that the revisionists "are collecting and banking obscure facts until the day we can rain them down on somebody's artistic parade" [1998:A64]. While this may be a little harsh, the revisionists do appear to take great joy in the challenge. Timing may have something to do with it, as the appearance of harsh condemnations coincided with the appearance of the United States *Foreign Policy* series from 1976 to 1984. It was also about this time as well that the British Public Records Office opened many of its records to the independent scholar.

What the revisionists' efforts discovered was considerable evidence that America's actions had not always been pure or consistently pragmatic. Basic to the revisionist interpretation is the acceptance of a reasonable American guilt for the war. There is also a degree of skepticism about the American pressure on the United Nations, as well as a high level of criticism of the United Nations itself. The causes for war in Korea, it suggests, were far more complex than altruistic determination to save the democratic Republic of South Korea.

Certainly the most outspoken of those representing this skepticism are Bruce Cumings and Jon Halliday. They have worked both independently and together. Cumings has researched deeply in materials that reflect the early years of American-Korean relations, and he has admirably reflected the theme of American responsibility. In his more outspoken moments he calls the Korean War an American creation. Reluctant to lay the blame for the outbreak at the doorstep of either the Communists or the American conservatives, he points to the lack, or inconsistency, of American policy. Many, both in the United States and in South Korea, disagreed with American involvement in South Korea and did what they could to keep us out. The pressure for involvement came from the American liberals and the Truman administration.

Cumings is at his best on the domestic roots of the conflict. Certainly much of the explanation for the eventual outbreak of war can be found in revolutionary activity going on in both North and South Korea, and the growing civil unrest throughout the country. In the final analysis, Cumings believes, the Communist Chinese had far better reasons for being at war in Korea than had the United States or, for that matter, the United Nations.

Their mutual work–Jon Halliday and Bruce Cumings, *The Unknown War: Korea* [1988]–is primarily an indictment of the United Nations and the United States. The views they represent, we are assured, emerge from "emancipated minds," full of new and secret material that has somehow been liberated. Jon Halliday agrees that the Korean War resulted from liberals who influenced the Truman administration. But he is equally as aware that much of the tension that led to the actual outbreak of war lay in the powerful class struggle going on in Korea.

Many revisionists suggest that neither the Democratic People's Republic of Korea, the Communist Chinese, nor the Soviet Union behaved quite as irrationally as it might have appeared. The Communists had reasons to fight that loomed far larger than the frequent national tendency to expand into the land of one's neighbors. Other works of the revisionist mode, like Donald Knox, *The Korean War: Uncertain Victory* [1988], defended American and British involvement but are much more sympathetic with the role of China and the plight of the Chinese soldier.

Peter Lowe's very useful work "The Significance of the Korean War in Anglo-American Relations" [1989] is often considered revisionist, for in it he provides a pragmatic, rather than an ideological, justification for American behavior. Lowe is not unreasonably harsh on America, yet he provides a critical look at the conflicting interests and diverse agendas of the major characters in the war. He acknowledges that British involvement was due less to an interest in Korea, or the United Nations, than to concern over what America was going to do.

The work of British historian and journalist Max Hastings is also critical, but he is not as quick to blame the United States as either Bruce Cumings or Jon Halliday. Hastings identifies both America's weakness, as well as its arrogance in dealing with the Korean people, as a cause of the war. But he is also cognizant that the situation was greatly confused by wider international misunderstandings. America had little experience in its role as a world leader. The tendency toward paternalism, and an insensitivity toward other nations created a problem in Korea, as it did later in Vietnam.

Hastings acknowledges that American action was greatly influenced by the fact the USSR was a powerful potential enemy, and that the fear of Soviet aggression was realistic. His point of view begins to reflect the movement of historical consideration beyond revisionism, and it reveals rather extensive research, including some oral testimony from Communist Chinese and North

Korean veterans. The increasing availability of materials from Communist archives makes it easier to answer some of the questions; also raises some significant new ones. Unfortunately, neither the North Korean, South Korean, nor Chinese have allowed independent investigation, though some scholars have had limited access. When more readily available, these materials should provide new–and most likely, different–accounts of the enemy's point of view.

Generalizing, we can identify two primary focuses in the revisionists' view. One is a willingness to look to some larger cause, whether a civil war or the international pressures emerging from the Cold War. They look both at the initial invasion of North Korean troops and at the later–and perhaps more significant–entry of the Communist Chinese in November 1950. The later event is addressed as more than an act of aggression, rather as the result of a powerful set of forces that included a threat to Chinese security, the development of divisions among domestic leadership, and a growth in international pressure [Hastings 1987:353].

Some revisionists swung farther than others. Those who swung the farthest are often referred to as operating in a "reverse heroic" mode that those in the orthodox position have things backwards. The "reverse heroic" reverses the roles played by the allies and the enemies. This view has unleashed a whole new generation of historical consideration.

POSTREVISIONISM

The term postrevisionism suggests the historical swing arising from the discovery of new material, increasing analysis, and views more sympathetic with the orthodox. It does not reflect a return to the orthodox but rather a new level of understanding that recognizes some inherent value in the earlier position. John Dillie's *Substitute for Victory* [1954] is an example of the new look at an old position. He concludes that the war in Korea was a good war, that "had to be fought."

Seeking to understand the context of events, pos-revisionists are inclined to see historical events as being more situational than heroic. While they do not ignore men of influence like President Truman or the impact of military leaders like Matthew B. Ridgway and MacArthur, they are more inclined to deal with them as persons with talent who nevertheless made human mistakes. The postrevisionists are more inclined to point to ignorance, inability, incompetence, and misunderstanding than they are to blame nations or support conspiracy theories.

So while identifying the mistakes committed by leaders like President Truman and General MacArthur, they do so with an evenhanded and contextual approach. The same is true of their handling of Communist China's leaders. They see in the Chinese military professional fighting men who conducted a well executed campaign. As well, they tend to acknowledge the national and international pressures behind the behavior of the various nations. They are thus not inclined to find single national causes; instead they concentrate on the complexities–like the great class struggle of the 1945-1950s, the powerful nationalism of the Chinese, and a host of previously misunderstood factors.

Two other generalized views merit some brief mention. One is called "Postrevisionists Synthesis. " This interpretation emerged in the 1970s but has not yet produced a great deal of material. Nevertheless, its proponents have increasing influence in the field. They share a rather eclectic view of the war's causes, speaking with a strong orthodox accent. One good example is Daniel Yergin, whose *Shattered Peace* [1977] divides political responsibility for the war in Korea between the United States and Russia. The postrevisionist synthesis view is that the narrative history must be reconsidered, not in terms of causation but to synthesize earlier views. The diversity of the agendas of the nations involved makes the conflict far too complex to be explained by any particular point of view. The postrevisionists seek instead a balanced, and nonjudgmental, interpretation by means of a "synthesis," which they have not yet provided.

The second is called "postmodernism." The term has been widely and diversely used; in fact, one might say, it has been thrown about so much as to lose much of its meaning. It is used here only to define what appears to be a phase of historical inquiry concerning the Korean War. The postmodernists are highly critical of the early orthodox points of view, especially American justifications. But they are also disturbed by the revisionist tendency to blame America for the outbreak of the war and for the failure of the peace. Postmodernism reflects a growing movement within the historical community to deal with what has been called the "balkanization" of history.

DISCIPLINES

While it is important to keep in mind the fashions of historical interpretations and how they relate to the writing of Korean War history, it is also important to acknowledge the differences in the various subjects (sometimes seen as disciplines) within the larger study of the war. Some areas–like the decision to go to war in Korea, the Inchon invasion, the role of the U.S. Marines, the disaster at Chosin, and the political implications of the armistice–have been looked at from a wide variety of directions.

Other areas, however, drawn little attention. Thus the materials we have about those aspects of the war do not have the advantage of historical critique–that is, presentation, criticism, and representation. Fortunately, it appears that once a subject is introduced, it begins, like the rolling snowball gathering more snow, to draw a large quantity–and often a good quality–of new investigations.

One area that has not received as much attention as it will need is the role of the various services. In most areas other than official histories, the roles of the army, navy, and air force have fallen far behind that of the marines. For what must be good reasons, but for reasons not yet identified, the materials produced about the armed services do not reflect the wide range of historical fashions–orthodoxy to postrevisionism–that are prevalent in other areas of inquiry. This does not mean there are no studies that have addressed the quality of the military's performance; there have been. But the central theme even of these has been the inadequacy of America's military preparation.

There is a rather large body of work concerning military commanders who suffered from "old war syndrome," a failure to recognize the altered character of the war they were fighting in Korea. D. Clayton James, in *Refighting the Last War* [1993], takes a balanced and serious look at this problem. Clay Blair, particularly, places a good deal of blame for military failure on General MacArthur, the X Corps commander Maj. Gen. Edmond Almond, and to a lesser degree on Eighth Army commander Gen. Walton Walker. Edwin P. Hoyt's *The Bloody Road to Pananmunjom* [1985] and John Toland's *In Mortal Combat* [1991] also place a good deal of responsibility on MacArthur, particularly for his splitting of Eighth Army and X Corps. Shelby Stanton's *America's Tenth Legion* [1989] rounds off this criticism and adds to it a heavy attack on Almond.

Edward Friedman suggests that the Communist Chinese intervention was the rational action of a nation trying to protect itself from General MacArthur and the American influence on the South Koreans. Friedman tends to agree with others who have suggested that the Far East commander was out of control. He believes MacArthur had far too much influence with the Joint Chiefs of Staff. Joseph Goulden, in *Korea: The Untold Story* of the War [1982], suggests that MacArthur's unbridled egotism and military failures were allowed to get thoroughly out of hand.

Following the Korean War, as the principal officers involved began to retire, several good memoirs and narratives appeared. Certainly these are an excellent source of factual information, and they are usually salted with personal agendas. One of the more significant of these is General J. Lawton Collins's *War in Peacetime: The History and Lessons of Korea* [1969]. He makes an interesting case as he looks at the Korean War from the position of the Joint Chiefs of Staff.

Max Hastings makes a rather serious charge against the individual American soldier, who in his opinion was ill-trained, ill-selected, and lacking in patriotism. This view, even though it sometimes appears, it is not widespread. T. R. Fehrenbach, in *This Kind of War* [1963], blames the army for behaving with a "civilian attitude." General S. L. A. Marshall, on the other hand, is very supportive of the American fighting man. In his *The River and the Gauntlet* [1953] he applauds the role of the foot-soldier, though he does level some criticism at middle command. His defense of General Walker and the Eighth Army's withdrawal is hard to believe.

If the Korean War is the forgotten war, then the U.S. Navy must be the forgotten service of the forgotten war. Little has been done to tell its story, even though the navy made a major contribution. The period of the Korean

War was a significant time for the navy in terms of mission and organization. Combining four commands and the Military Sea Transportation Service, Naval Forces Far East, was involved from the beginning and right up to the end. It made many unacknowledged efforts and there has been little has been said about the fascinating story of submarines in the Korean War.

It is safe to call the U.S. Marines the most written about of the services in Korea. The marines, for good reason, are usually in the middle of things, and thus accounts of their service are full of adventure. More than a dozen good works, in addition to the official histories, have appeared about the marines in Korea. Among these are Robert Leckie, *The March to Glory,* [1960], and Allen Millet, *Semper Fidelis: The History of the United States Marine Corps* [1991]. There are, however, still some significant parts of the role of the Marines in Korea that have not been adequately covered.

The many aspects of the air war in Korea have been addressed, but again, there is much left to cover. All of these air support units–U.S. Navy squadrons, the marine aircraft, and the U. S. Air Force–all need more inquiry. There have been two or three early classic works, including Richard P. Hallion, *The Naval Air War in Korea* [1986] which provides an excellent beginning. Because of the broad interest in aircraft, the planes involved in the Korean War have received more attention than the services. So far, no really competent scholarly work has been done from Communist materials. This means that no matter how carefully men like Robert F. Futrell pursue their efforts, in works like *The United States Air Force in Korea, 1950 -1953* [1983] the full story has yet to be told.

Within the four major services were many units, support outfits, and special assignment troops that have not received much coverage. Just to touch on this area, there are some great stories to be told about the participation of groups like the Rangers, the combat engineers, and the airborne troops. The whole question of supply along a route nearly five thousand miles from the source of supply, is an important and interesting story. The whole logistical and supply system was of great significance, but other than some good work by James A. Huston (*Guns and Butter, Powder and Rice: U. S. Army Logistics in the Korean War* [1989]) and a few others, the story is generally unknown.

Popular interest in the weapons and vehicles of war has resulted in a wide variety of illustrated books published. One important part of the consideration of the role of weapons has to deal with combat use. As noted above, S. L. A. Marshall has done some interesting work on the percentage of troops actually firing their weapons in anger. This issue needs more study and analysis.

As mentioned, many of the important battles in the Korean War await consideration and analysis. Among those that have been well depicted are Inchon and Chosin, as well as the Pusan perimeter and the battles along the Naktong. What is especially lacking, however, is a series of good monographs on the hill war, that period from about November 1951 to the Armistice. This period of small unit fighting witnessed some of the most desperate, and costly, fighting of the war.

While there have been some fine studies about nuclear issues during the Korean War, especially in conjunction with the larger framework of the Cold War, there is very little on the military side. Certainly the decisions, and the forces behind it, reflect political rather than military considerations, but there is considerable evidence that the military requested atomic weapons, that they were brought into Korea (or at least to an advanced American military base), and that there were exercises practicing dropping "the bomb" on North Korean or Chinese territory. The military side of this issues remains primarily untold.

Another issue about which there is no clear understanding is the American introduction of biological warfare in Korea. Charged with the crime by the Communist Chinese, the United States has always denied it. However, a recent study by Stephen Endicott and Edward Hagerman, *The United States and Biological Warfare: Secrets from the Early Cold War and Korea* [1998], has raised this question once again. The Chinese accused the United States of dropping live insects, rotten fish, and rodents, among other things, recent inquiries suggest that there might well be some substance to this charge. There appears to be little doubt that some units, under certain circumstances, used some form of biological weapons against North Korea. What, why, how, and with what effect are questions that must be addressed in depth if we are to understand what happened in Korea or its effect on us today.

Much of what has been taught about the Korean War, when it *has* been taught, tends to focus on the United Nations. The significance of this war, the first major military commitment of the United Nations, is important. But the complexity of both the involvement and its purpose will require considerable research and discussion. There is not a great deal of understanding about what the commitment was, which nations were involved, and what share of the burden, militarily and economically, they carried. Little has even been attempted in this area.

Besides the wide variety of national interests, there are the questions of the interrelatedness of forces under United Nations command. Many of the nations involved produced official histories, or at least national commentaries, concerning their experiences in Korea. What is available is well identified in Lester H. Brune, *The Korean War: Handbook of the Literature and Research* [1996], a highly valuable research aid. In this study are chapters on Canada, Great Britain, Australia, New Zealand, Japan, South Korea, China, and the Soviet Union. Still, there is very little on the details of the multinational contribution. Little, as well, is available on the makeup, functioning, logistics, language difficulties, command structures, and the rest of the vast story of what became known as the United Nations forces.

DOMESTIC

We are indebted to Bruce Cumings and others who have raised questions about the degree to which the war in Korea was a continuation of the civil wars that had been raging, in one form or another, for decades. This was a situation that the United States should have understood it should have known that sooner or later conflict would erupt between North and South. Few have taken a serious look at the internal and revolutionary difficulties in South Korea. Another area for further study is the impact of the three million or so refugees who left North Korea after the division in 1946.

In contrast, the international character of the Korean War makes it necessary to seek some broader international understanding. One significant move has been to supplement what American documentation is available with that of other involved nations. This includes the increasing available records from some Communist nations. Ryo Hagiwara, *The Korean War: The Conspiracies by Kim Il Sung and MacArthur,* tells the story from the point of the Japanese communists. One of the better international examinations is William J. Stueck, *The Korean War: An International History* [1995].

Another good look at the international diplomatic causes of the Cold War and of Korea is Melvyn P. Leffler's *A Preponderance of Power: National Security, Truman Administration, and the Cold War* [1992]. Leffler suggests that the United States greatly overreacted to Soviet behavior–that the America's reaction reflected a real lack of understanding of the world situation and of the conflicting national goals. Looking at Western foreign policy in the light of Korea political history, James I. Matray, in *The Reluctant Crusade: American Foreign Policy in Korea, 1941 - 1950* [1991], provides considerable insights. An area that is rich in history but of which there has been only limited coverage for the period of the Korean War is the role of the CIA, SIS, and other intelligence agencies. The war in Korea had its clandestine side, and it both benefitted and suffered from a rather active intelligence service. The recent study by William Breuer, *Shadow Warriors* [1996], is an excellent first look. This may be one of the last areas in which a good study will be conducted, and we must wait to determine both the effectiveness and capabilities of the network of spies and secrets.

In the last few years work has been done on the effect of the Korean War on the American domestic scene. This would include two excellent works, David Halberstam's *The 1950s* [1993] and a recent study, Lisle A. Rose, *The Cold War Comes to Main Street: America in 1950* [1999]. The wider interest, however, is not only with America in the 1950s but with how the Korean War affected life on Main Street, whether in London or Bejing.

One way of looking at the homefront is to start with the role of presidents. Certainly, works on Harry S. Truman and Dwight D. Eisenhower provide an understanding of the domestic scene. The growing amount of research that has been done on both these presidents reflects not only the war years but their influence on prewar and postwar America. In this area, revisionist Barton Berstein's "Politics and Policies of the Truman Administration" is a major contribution. A balanced description of the era can be found in John Diggins, *The Proud Decade* [1988].

During the last thirty years, history itself has undergone some major analysis and revision. What has been happening has been likened, in the words of the highly insightful David Ashley, to a "balkanization of culture and society" [1997:453]. The essence of history, as well as the influence of historians, is now seen more and more within the context of race, gender, ethnic environment, and a whole array of new social movements.

The influence of postmodern theory has altered not so much the narrative nature of history as the structure of history. Postmodernism is not so much "a thought in its own right but rather . . . a significant symptom, a function of the increasing difficulties in thinking of such a set of interrelationships in a complicated society" [Ashley, David 1997:back cover].

This is not the place for a detailed discussion of the issue, but we must at least acknowledge the growing gap in historical understanding between what *signifies* and what *is signified*. The difficulty in seeing, or projecting, any objective reality–be it God, "the Force," or fate–as a constant in history means, in the postmodern view, that historians are more and more dependent on self-referential explanations. Each (all) of these self-referential explanations must be considered as worthy as any other explanation. The changing character of historiography is yet to be addressed, but when it is, there may well be a serious change in the approach that has been the mainstay of most narrative histories of the Korean War.

There are not much interest in historiography among American historians, so it should come as no surprise that there are few historiographies of the Korean War. Of those available, certainly Robert Swartout Jr. "American Historians and the Outbreak of the Korean War: An Historiographical Essay," *Asian Quarterly* (1979), is one of the best. Also of value is Karunakar Gupta's "How Did the Civil War Begin?"[1972], which discusses studies of the beginning aspects of the war. Philip West's "Interpreting the Korean War," in *American Historical Review* [1989], is an excellent analysis of six major works. In it he provides an brief but informative history of the history of the Korean War. One interesting point is the degree to which many articles and books are extensions or popularizations of materials first introduced by Roy E. Appleman in his official and unofficial series on the Korean War.

A good number of what is available in English are sympathetic toward the Republic of Korea and with the positions taken by the United States and the United Nations. Obviously the degree of understanding is limited by restrictions imposed by the researchers' inability to read and understand languages of nation being studied. Few scholars enjoy the language skills necessary. While a reading knowledge of Chinese, Korean, and Russian is not necessary for the more general studies about the war in Korea, it becomes essential if serious studies are going to probe deeper, in a serious study. Fortunately, an increasing number of scholars who are studying the Korean War are acquiring those skills.

It should come as no great surprise to anyone that the histories of the

Korean War tell us as much about the times in which they were written as they do the subject about which they were written. The conditions under which scholars write or participants remember add to the bias and subjectivity of their works. It is equally true that the environment of inquiry, as identified by previous work, affects their work. Thus it is often the case that to learn about a period it is helpful to read the historians of the period. Even when they are addressing another topic, they are conveying the character of the times and beliefs (prejudices) in which they write.

Perhaps the best conclusion to this discussion about the growing influence of revisionism are the words of historian Philip West:

Conceived out of the smaller heroism, some of the interpretations of the Korean War, whether in English, Korean, or Chinese, may–and perhaps should–be forgotten within the next few decades. Given the depth of emotions that still surround the Korean War and the lack of access to Korean and Chinese archives, it may be some time before an interpretation is conceived in the higher historiography, penned with an even hand, and credible to more than one side can be expected to appear [1989:96].

Chapter 10

The Fighting Just Stopped

Those who are able to start a war are sometimes to
discover that they lack the power to stop it.

Darian Cobb

Sometimes, in order to understand how a war begins it is necessary to know
something of how it ends. Fred Ikle, who served the United States both as
Undersecretary of Defense for Policy and as director of the United States Arms
Control and Disarmament Agency, considered this in his book *Every War
Must End* [Ikle 1991]. He suggests that no one seems to have given a great deal
of consideration to how the war might have been stopped. It was hard to
determine, in fact, who had authority to negotiate peace.

The American people were hardly more aware of the disheartening charades
played out at the negotiation table than they were of the miscalculations that
first led to war. The American press moved back and forth between
unwarranted optimism and unrestrained pronouncements of doom and
destruction. The simple truth was that for the Communist's, their participation
in the cease-fire talks was but one phase in the larger war. They negotiated
with the same careful skill they used in their military campaigns. Both the
ideological leaders, Lenin and Mao, were proponents of the doctrine of
protracted conflict. In that process, historical inevitability must be tempered
by the practical acknowledgment that a nation should never attempt a decisive
action when victory was uncertain. The Communists knew, as the United
Nations was slowly discovering, that vast military force was not necessary to
establish favorable conditions for negotiation. The negotiated extension of the
war was the obvious outcome of the Communists' understanding that neither
a final decisive blow nor a forced end to the war would serve their long-term
interests.

The road to the armistice was a difficult one. The negotiations were a
counterbalance to the fighting, and on more than one occasion the dictates of
military necessity fell victim to political considerations. The nations

represented at the table had defined agendas; their goals were less well defined. But for a good portion of the discussions, the primary goal was not an armistice.

The United Nations failed to destroy the North Korean People's Army during the initial phase of the war. Therefore, the allies of South Korea were not able to impose a peaceful unification on the peninsula. In an effort to accomplish its purpose, United Nations unleashed its forces across the 38th Parallel in a drive on the Yalu River. This act, which both General MacArthur and the Joint Chiefs of Staff saw as a military necessity, proved to be a political liability. Conditions were soon so altered, and the price had risen so high, that the unification of Korea became a secondary concern.

While it is easy to look back on the decision to cross the 38th Parallel with disfavor, or, misunderstanding, it is important to remember that the United States and the United Nations saw Korea as a single entity. As far as they were concerned, the 38th Parallel was an administrative, rather than a national, boundary. Crossing this line did not carry the same connotation for the United Nations as it did for North Korea and Communist China. thus the decision was made in a much different context than that in which it was viewed by others.

The war was not very old when the United Nations established a Cease-fire Group, in the hope that some sort of conclusion might be reached. The group was based on the cease-fire resolution passed on December 14, 1950, sponsored by the Arab-Asian block. It had called upon the secretary - general of the General Assembly to appoint three people to determine a basis on which a cease-fire in Korea could be arranged. However, the North Koreans seemed to have little interest in an armistice. The Chinese, for their part, considered the group to be illegal. because the People's Republic of China, lacking UN membership, had not been involved in its formation.

While it was fairly easy to identify the Democratic People's Republic of Korea as the instigator of the war, it was far more difficult to find parties that really wanted the war to end. In many respects, all nations involved seemed to feel they might be profited from its continuation. On the other hand, each also had some reasons for wanting to see the war end. The North Koreans, at least Kim Il Sung, had assumed that the war would be over in a few days. As it dragged on it became increasingly difficulty to meet its costs.

The negotiations with the Communists were handled primarily by the United States, and by military personnel. The other nations of the United Nations were generally excluded. Prime Minister Winston Churchill asked to have his conservative government included in the discussions, but it never was.

It is hard to know just how committed the United States was to a settlement. There is certainly no evidence that the United States was anxious to meet the Communist demands, and the United Nations was as inclined to suspend talks as were the Chinese. More than twenty-two months into the armistice talks, John Foster Dulles, the American's secretary of state, still felt that it was necessary to give the Chinese a licking before any move to get out of the war.

Premier Chou En-lai officially rejected the United Nations cease-fire proposal, and on January 3, 1951, the Cease-fire Group had to report to the General Assembly that it had failed. In an effort to get discussions off the ground, the United States voted in favor of a resolution that allowed the talks to include of other items outstanding in the Far East. This too was rejected.

The communist belligerents, which at the moment had the United Nations troops on the run, argued that the whole purpose of the "cease-fire before negotiations" was an effort to provide the American troops breathing room. In this belief, the Communists rejected the various proposals and condemned the five points that the United Nations had developed as the basis for negotiations. The United Nations was reduced to forming the United Nations Good Offices Committee. This committee was given the vague assignment of working toward a peace effort.

While the United Nations was considering an early armistice, Pak Jin-mok, a member of the South Korean Workers Party, was active. He felt that it was important for the South Korean people to initiate an armistice effort to avoid further destruction to their nation. He made a secret effort to bring this about, but it failed. He, like several other South Koreans who tried to bring about peace, was accused of treason or of working with the Democratic People's Republic of Korea. The repercussions were more than expected, and they probably did much to delay any legitimate talks. At this point, distrust among the politically inspired Koreans was too massive to overcome.

In early March 1951, President Truman proposed that the United Nations broadcast an invitation for cease-fire discussions. The incentive would be that the alternative would be a more expanded military effort by the United Nations. General MacArthur was notified of Truman's plan on March 20. Before the administration could execute its plans, however, General MacArthur issued his own ultimatum to the Chinese, calling for an immediate surrender. He hinted that if the Chinese did not return to the table, they ran the risk of attack on Communist China itself. It was this imposition of his will on the peace plans of the president, as much as anything, that led to Truman's demand for the general's dismissal. The Communist Chinese, who were militarily dominant at the time, rejected the ultimatum.

The original U.S. idea for a cease-fire was to restore the status quo–that is, to expel the invading troops of North Korea. But this soon changed. this aim was abandoned, and President Truman defined a new expectation. The goal of a cease-fire became the destruction of the government of Kim Il Sung. Despite its vast nature, this change was not communicated to the American people. The drive to the Yalu River was presented as the natural outcome of the successful invasion of Inchon.

It was increasingly evident that if overthrowing the Pyongyong regime was his was what America wanted, it could not be accomplished with less than a full military commitment. However, "containment of communism" and a show of force in the face of Soviet expansion, could be accomplished with a well-negotiated armistice.

The Truman administration took a backdoor approach through individual contact. On May 31, 1951, a private meeting was arranged between George F. Kennan, a State Department Soviet expert on leave of absence, and Jacob A. Malik, the Soviet UN ambassador. The two men had a history of friendly relations. The result of this diplomatic connection was a second meeting, on June 5, 1951. Following these discussions, Ambassador Malik delivered a radio address on June 23, 1951, entitled "The Price of Peace." He provided unofficial support for the opening of armistice talks. The Soviet spokesman was clear, however, that since the Soviets were not involved in the fighting, they could not participate in the discussions.

It must be acknowledged that even at this early point there was a rather wide division of opinion in the United States. The dichotomy lay between those who wanted a peaceful settlement as quickly as possible, and those who still saw a need to punish, if eliminate, the communist nations of China and North Korea. When the tide of the war changed and the United Nations held, the effort to start peace discussions was again considered.

General Ridgway, after he replaced MacArthur in April 1951, was instructed to offer talks. Ridgway broadcast an invitation to peace discussions to the leaders of the Chinese People's Volunteer Army and the North Korean People's Army. He approached the suggestion very carefully, being sure to avoid the harsh criticism of the Communist nations that General MacArthur had included in his communications. Ridgway suggested that both sides might profit from a discussion, and recommended a meeting aboard the *Jutlandia,* a Dutch hospital ship then located at Wonsan.

The response came rather quickly, giving somewhat would prove to be false hope. The statement, received July 1, was authorized by Kim Il Sung and Peng-The huai of the Chinese People's Volunteer Army. They agreed to a meeting of delegates but rejected the location; they suggested the talks begin at the village of Kaesong. Kaesong was located on the 38th Parallel, and it was about to fall to United Nations troops.

Kaesong, some thirty-five miles northwest of Seoul, was accepted by President Truman and Joint Chiefs of Staff, despite the objections of General Ridgway. This compliant reaction, as well as several other concessions made during the first three months of the negotiations, led the Communist negotiators to believe the United States was much more interested in a cease-fire that they were. Kaesong was still in the hands of Communists troops, and the UN delegates had to pass through armed defenders to get to the talks. At the insistence of Admiral C. Turner Joy, America's chief negotiator, a five-mile security zone was created through which the United Nations Command negotiators would have unrestricted movement. The Communists accepted these terms, but there were several violations.

The armistice talks began on July 10, 1951, between the United Nations Command, the Chinese Communist forces, and the North Korean People's

Army. The Communist delegates proved tough from the start. However, by the 26th an agenda had been agreed on. That it would be a long and frustrating process was, however, already apparent. In less than a month, the Chinese claimed there had been an ambush near Kaesong; they suspended talks and demand an apology for the violation of the "safe zone." It seemed that the talks were over before they had really begun. More than a month passed before the United States took the initiative. At that point Ambassador Alan G. Kirk met with the Soviet foreign minister, Andrei Y. Vishinsky.

Ambassador Kirk urged the Soviet diplomat to use his good offices to persuade the Chinese and North Koreans to resume the cease-fire talks. Vyshinsky apparently favored a cease-fire, but he expressed opposition to the United Nations position on voluntary repatriation (discussed below). He felt that the prisoners of war should be returned to nations of origin, regardless of their wishes. He did offer to postpone the prisoner talks until after a cease-fire could be set in operation. If the United States had been open to this, there might well have been an end to the fighting even without concession on this issue. The degree of Soviet influence is not well documented, but by October 22, 1951, the warring parties had signed an agreement on a security zone, and three days later talks were resumed in the small village of Panmunjom.

In September and October, military successes achieved by the United Nations helped to define the degree to which it would use force to support negotiations. Admiral Joy complained that "the United Nations command forces were not allowed to attack their enemies in the most effective manner nor with the most effective weapons. In consequence, the United Nations command could not exert the decisive military pressure of which it was capable"[Bacahus: 545].

The United Nations representative proposed that the armistice demarcation line be accepted as the Demilitarized Zone (DMZ), on the condition that the remaining items in an armistice agreement be worked out within thirty days. By December 3, however, the delegates had moved the question of cease-fire inspections to subdelegates. The discussions dragged on, and the issues were still being argued when, on December 27, the proposed demarcation line agreement made at Panmunjom expired. As the front stabilized and the fighting was reduced to a series of bloody static battles, events of the war came to be driven by the political discussions going on at the time.

The major issue under consideration was more political than military. From November 1951 to June 1953, the issue defying compromise was that of the distribution of prisoners of war. The Bureau of Psychological Warfare, a civilian agency, had proposed voluntary repatriation of prisoners. The idea reflected the views of President Truman, who was personally concerned about the fate of captives, forced to return to their countries against their wishes. For the captured Communists to stay in the South, rather than returning to communism would have had a favorable effect on the defector program. It would also make surrender far more meaningful, and potentially advantageous, to the individual.

The United Nations, primarily reflecting President Truman's adamant view, made voluntary repatriation the keystone of discussion. The United Nations declared that it was taking a moral stand. It might have been so for some, but in reality the position was a political demand that reflected the popular view that communism was an "enforced" belief. The position of the United Nations was defined in a January 2, 1952, proposal for voluntary repatriation of POWs. The Communists, six days later and apparently without much consideration, rejected this proposal. By the end of the month the question of POW release was, as noted above, sent to subdelegates for detailed discussion.

The Chinese and North Korean delegate walked an interesting line combining consistent disagreement on issues, and encouragement of the continuation of the cease-fire talks themselves. During the first year both the North Korean and Chinese suffered several military defeats, but the Communists continued the discussions in a manner that, had it succeeded, would have produced victory–that is the withdrawal of all foreign troops.

Thus they continually blocked solutions to issues but made efforts l efforts to keep the talks alive. In early January 1952, they suggested that the Soviet Union be one of the neutral nations conducting cease-fire inspections. In April of that year, the Communist delegation suggested that a check be made among present POWs to see how many persons would be repatriated if it were voluntary.

The United Nations embarked on Operation Scatter, a quick count of the POWs in its hands, and reported that seventy thousand Communists had indicated that they did not want to return home. After that report the Chinese refused to consider repatriations. However, they dropped their demands that the Soviet Union be a neutral nation on the inspection team. In July they reaffirmed the demand that all Chinese POWs be returned.

Several other nations made proposals to bring about some sort of cease-fire. Great Britain, though an American ally from the beginning, was worried that the United States might allow events in Korea to redirect its concern from the primary problems in Europe. Thus the British tried on several occasions to mediate with the Soviet Union to bring about a settlement. The United States responded with anger. After the Chinese invasion the British suggested that discussions be expanded to include American opposition to the admission of China to the United Nations, as well its recognition of Nationalist China. The British were joined in a variation on this proposal, a five-point peace program, by India and Canada. The United States did not like it. As it turned out, neither did the Chinese. The British continued in its attempts until October 1952, when it supported the V. K. Krishna Menon POW settlement. The United States nearly allowed this to cause a break in Anglo-American relations.

In September 1952, the Mexican government had offered a plan proposed by Luis Padilla Nervo, the Mexican ambassador to the United Nations. He proposed a POW settlement based on sending those who resisted repatriation to neutral sites and keeping them there until the decision about reparations was made. But it had become evident in a series of private meetings that neither the Communist Chinese nor the North Koreans trusted Mexico, and the proposal was no more successful than was the October Menon or the November Peruvian proposals. Seeing no progress, the United Nations declared an indefinite recess of the Panmunjom truce talks.

Gen. Mark Clark, the Eighth Army commander during this period, wanted to military reasons to avoid an armistice. He felt the Chinese were seeking a break in order to rebuild their strength for a renewal of fighting.

The frustration was heightened by the fact that the military men rather than diplomats conducted the armistice talks. Also, the delegates were not able to negotiate from a position of strength. As long as the enemy was not facing defeat, any armistice could be little other than political. It became even more difficult when the orders to the negotiators no longer came from the State Department but president, by way of the Joint Chiefs of Staff.

The whole idea of limited war has its drawbacks. One of the more obvious is that in a limited war the more powerful of the combatants has a liability, whereas the cases the lesser military power has a variety of options. To be strong is not necessarily an advantage in a war in which victory is not the goal. The cease-fire option is always to the lesser power's advantage.

The period between December 1950 and the middle of June 1951 was one of movement back and forth representing the relative strengths of each side. It was the decision of the United Nations–primarily the United States–to bring this war of movement to a halt in order to place the decision more profoundly at the negotiation table [Bacahus:545]. The Americans decided that the casualty rates show that "relatively static combat favored the communist forces regarding loss ratios and significantly reduced the total number of casualties, the factor about which the United Nations command was most concerned. Thus both parties became more amenable to a stalemate and to negotiations in preference to any large-scale resumption of the seesaw offensive war"[Bacahus:545].

Traditionally, negotiations are conducted when all parties reasonably expect that the others will act with reason and are interested in considering proposals. This was not necessarily the case in Korea. At least during some periods of discussion, the Communist goal was not a cease-fire but the value–propaganda and otherwise–of the continuation of the talks. While the United States would survive as a political entity even under the worst of scenarios in Korea, there was some question whether the new and still not totally stable Communist governments could lose militarily and still retain political viability.

Also, and though this most probably was not the reason for it, the dismissal of General MacArthur, who had been pushing an attack on the Chinese mainland, most likely encouraged the Chinese to believe that the danger of an American invasion had lessened.

Premier Mao was concerned about the implications of a stalemate at the 38th Parallel, because it did not settle the question. As late as February 1953, Mao would announce that as long as the Americans demanded voluntary repartition, China would fight on. There was, however, an obvious shift in his thinking. At least it was outwardly Mao speaking–there may well have been considerable pressure on him. The shift appears to have followed Mao's realization that the war in Korea could not be won quickly. He urged his forces to win it "with delay" if necessary, but win. He finally came to the point where he believed that his forces would not be able to drive the United Nations from Korea [Zhang 1993:12].

Certainly the death of Joseph Stalin in March 1953 had something to do with the decision to accept an armistice. The members of the Soviet Politburo were deeply involved in their own political questions. They rejected the Chinese request for more weapons and economic assistance, and in the main they suggested a peaceful solution to all international conflicts. The Russian reluctance to support China gave Mao pause. But it was still his hope that fear of a Soviet reprisal would prevent the United States from using the atomic bomb.

The Chinese did establish the "legality" of the 38th Parallel and thus reduced the risk of further conflict on that issue. In essence, while still dealing the question of POWs, the repartition–without United Nations or American interference–was settled. In June 1953, the Communists agreed to voluntary repatriation of prisoners of war–primarily agreeing to what the United Nations had proposed before–and a month later the armistice was signed. But the ability, or perhaps the determination, of the Communists to procrastinate had been very costly in terms of casualties. Both sides suffered heavily, so heavily that the president might have had considerable difficulty waiting, if they had been anticipated. The pressure was on Truman to end the war, and he was having trouble retaining public support.

"Nothing," wrote Fred Ikle, "is more divisive for a government than having to make peace at the price of major concessions. The process of ending a war almost inevitably evokes an intense internal struggle if it means abandoning an ally or giving up popularly accepted objectives" [Ikle 1991:58].

The continued casualty rates had a greater impact on the folks back home. Certainly U.S. government officials sensed a weakening support for the war at home and among member nations. When it became obvious that there was no victory in sight, what little public support had been generated was lost. The president, facing defeat, decided not to run again for office. This weakened the administration's position. The succeeding Eisenhower administration certainly sent word that it was willing to expand the war geographically. The much larger and more violent protests of the Vietnam War era overshadowed the Korea concerns, but large, and in a few cases violent, antiwar marches, sponsored by the American Peace Crusade, occurred in San Francisco and Chicago in 1951 and 1952.

In February 1953, the United Nations suggested an exchange of sick and wounded prisoners. Surprisingly, it was considered. It was while this was being discussed that Joseph Stalin died. In mid-March, Georgi Malenkov spoke in support of a cease-fire in Korea, and by the last of March the Communists had accepted the proposal; Chou En-lai broadcast that he would be willing to discuss a proposed settlement on wounded and sick POWs.

Operation Little Switch, the exchange of the sick and wounded, was conducted under Present Eisenhower's threat of escalating military operations against North Korea and China. On April 11, the operation was approved, and by May 3 the primary exchange had been made. In this atmosphere, the talks at Panmunjom resumed. Lt. Gen. Nam Il advanced an eight-point POW settlement proposal. Secretary of State Dulles warned China, through the neutral state of India, that the United States might use atomic weapons if the current UN proposal was rejected. On June 4, 1953, the Communists accepted the May 25, 1953, United Nations POW settlement.

Why, one wonders in hindsight, did the Communists now accept these terms? It was not military pressure in the field, for that was no greater than it had been a year earlier. Nor does it appear that the decision was based on the threat of nuclear attack, for too had been made, and ignored, once before. In fact some of the most intense fighting occurred virtually at the same time the Communists were accepting cease-fire terms. Once again, the matter was political and complex. The death of Stalin not only freed commitments made to him and by him but brought a period of infighting in the Kremlin. On the other hand, the election of Eisenhower produced a president of the United States determined to arrive at a peace settlement though negotiations yet he willing to enforce a settlement. Also, of significance, but it is not clear just how much, was the release of Chiang Kai-shek's forces to act on their own initiative. This release, offered by Eisenhower's administration, freed the Nationalist Chinese to take their own initiative against mainland China.

By early June the Communists had approved the concept of voluntary repatriations and by the 17th had accepted a revised demarcation line. But the complexities of the various national agendas came into play here. South Korea had, it felt, the most to lose from such an armistice.

President Syngman Rhee did not favor the cease-fire. He did not want the war to end at this point. He was opposed to any armistice that left the question of unification unsettled, because of the danger that such a peace treaty would bring unbearable pressure on him, for any government that agrees to a peace settlement risks losing the support it had during the war. Rhee saw in the peace settlement not only a failure to punish North Korea,, but a threat to his own domestic leadership.

The political considerations involved in the agreement on conditional peace were the same as those concerning the war's original goals. Thus peace efforts affect not only the will to fight but the initial values of the goals for which fighting occurred. Usually–that is, prior to the Korean War–the disadvantage of armistice considerations was that they weakened the will to fight, particularly among citizen soldiers.

To prevent an armistice from being signed, and probably out of concern for the North Korean prisoners he envisioned otherwise being returned to communist hands, President Rhee released twenty-seven thousand POWs from the camps under his control. The majority of the prisoners melted into the countryside. There was every reason to believe that this action would halt the peace effort, but both the United States and Communists seemed to want the agreement, and the signing went ahead. It became necessary for the United States to make some concessions and to take drastic actions to convince President Rhee.

The release of the North Korean prisoners made one thing much clearer, however: the Chinese had not been concerned about Communists prisoners as such but primarily about Chinese ones. Both sides at the table were angry about Rhee's action ,and they agreed to recess at Panmunjom. At this point the U.S. options included Operation Everready. However, this plan to take over the South Korean government by military force and replace the president with a more agreeable leader was not executed. Rhee was aware that if he created more trouble the United States would no longer support him. After promises of mutual assistance, Rhee agreed, on July 10, 1953, not to disrupt the armistice agreement. There is little doubt, as well, that the fact the Communist Chinese had concentrated its forces against the ROK during the last series of attacks had shown Rhee that he could not go it alone.

The arguments between the opposing forces continued right up until the signing. Finally, it was agreed that the senior delegates, Gen. William K. Harrison Jr. and Gen. Nam Il would sign at the negotiation area at 10:00 A.M. on July 27, 1953. Those who were to sign were the military leaders–Gen. Mark Clark for the United Nations, and Kim Il Sung and Peng The-huai for their respective people's armies. After resolving a dispute about which door to enter, the document was signed without comment, to be effective twelve hours later. President Rhee did not sign, nor did any representative of the Republic of South Korea. The press, called in to observe the signing , reported that those involved looked like they were starting, rather than ending, a war.

WHO WON?

The United States had made its stand against Communist aggression. Communist China, which suffered enormous casualties and a continued rift with the United Nations, nevertheless had accumulated international prestige and national solidarity. It established itself as a worthy peer to the Soviet Union among communist nations. The USSR, it appears, was one of the larger losers, in terms of expectations. North Korea had failed to unite the peninsula, but then so had South Korea. Nationalist China may or may not have come out ahead, but at least it had been saved from what probably would have been a 1950 invasion from the mainland. The overall winner most probably was

Japan, which—less than five years after massive defeat—emerged as a free nation with economic strength and almost unlimited potential.

Bin Yo makes an excellent case that Communist China paid a very high price for its decision to enter into the Korean War. Among the more obvious reasons was the economic difficulty it created. For despite Moscow's promise to help, Mao Tse-tung ended up paying for most of the materials he received. But the most serious outcome, with the advantage of hindsight, is most probably that the events of the Korean War planted the seeds of future trouble in China's relations with Moscow.

When peace terms fail to meet the expectations that accompanied the decision to go to war, those who supported the original effort feel betrayed and consider the peacemakers as traitors. "The concessions required for peace, however, are not the only cause of internal disagreement. When the fighting comes to an end, the heavy toll that the war had taken—like a debt that comes due—may suddenly contribute to dissensions at home. Indeed, after prolonged and costly fighting, not only the losing nations but also the victors are often torn by political upheavals" [Ikle 1991].

When it becomes necessary for a nation to end a war, it is often equally necessary that those who have been in charge to be removed. The people of a nation tend to believe, as did MacArthur, that "war's objective is victory—not prolonged indecision. In war, there is no substitute for victory." To bring the fighting to an end, one nation or the other must reconsider and reinterpret its war aims. That, in turn, calls for a reevaluation of its military expectations. These are never simple nor is the reevaluation ever very clear. Those involved in the resulting concessions are wise if they realize that they themselves will eventually be the ultimate victims of the war. This was seen with Winston Churchill at the completion of World War II, certainly in Truman's decision not to run, and perhaps in President Lyndon Johnson's decision against another term.

But in a limited war, or one ended before the success of its primary goals, the people of the nation also suffer, and in the suffering the betrayal will cut into the nation's memory. It was nearly forty years before the Korean War Veterans Association was organized (1985), or the Chosin Few (1983), or the Korean War Veterans International (1986). It was more than forty years before a national monument was created. It is as if it was necessary to understand the wounds of Vietnam, maybe even to heal them, before consideration could be given to the Korean War.   It should not come as a surprise that during the awful national experience in Vietnam, there was little talk of Korea. Yet it is not hard to compare the two in terms of lessons learned or not learned. But it is interesting to consider how the second Asian war might have been fought differently, or perhaps not at all, had people been more aware of the Korean War.

American presidents have often referred to the Korean War in terms of victory. They talk of the American military's holding the line. They use the marines at the Chosin Reservoir or the preservation of South Korea as illustrations. Remembering with increasing nostalgia the days when we were Number One in the world we sometimes find it hard to remember the time this dream was tested by reality. Nevertheless this is a war that needs to be acknowledged. It was too costly to be forgotten.

> Our nation honors her sons
> And daughters who answered
> The call to defend a country
> They did not know, and a people
> They had never met.

> Korean Memorial

Chapter 11

The Wrong War

> The Korean War is an unattractive task which most Americans
> are more than happy to have slip through the cracks of history.

> Joseph Goulden

When considering Korea, Gen. Douglas A. MacArthur told members of his staff in 1947 he did not want any part of the messy situation there. That same year, Lt. Gen. John R. Hodge, the military governor of Korea during the occupation, expounded to the Joint Chiefs of Staff expounded on his frustration: "I have always been aware that Korea has been low on the agenda, but it may soon reach the point of explosion." The Department of State and the Department of Defense carried on endless discussions about Korea and never came to any good solution. The question became more disturbing when Mao Tse-tung was able to centralize China under communists control, having defeated America's favorite nationalist, Chiang Kai-shek. In the end, the need for economy ruled supreme, and it was considered necessary to reduce the cost of maintaining men in, and providing economic aid to, Korea.

In expressing his concern about an expanded Chinese involvement in the Korean War, Omar Bradley, General of the Army and chairman of the Joint Chiefs of Staff, declared that a war with China would be "the wrong war, in the wrong place, at the wrong time, and with the wrong enemy" [Goulden 1982:xv]. This quote is often used to describe the Korean War; though not directly concerned with Korea, it does provide a good description of the feeling many shared it.

It is not difficult to acknowledge that Korea, either the Democratic People's Republic of Korea (North) or the Republic of Korea (South), is not a very good place for a war. It was also not a place with which Americans identified. While the United States had had an early connection with Korea, including an "invasion" in 1870, it was not highly valued by America or Americans. There were few Koreans living in America, and the United States had never done much to understand or appreciate the Korean culture.

"Yellow peril" legislation had prevented many Koreans from emigrating to the United States. The Korean Peninsula, though in places beautiful and enchanting, had very little strategic value to the U.S. military establishment. The harshness of the Korean geography caused many a soldier to wonder why in the world anyone would want to fight over it. The bulk of the country is covered with mountains and hills. The transportation and communication systems were crude, and after three years of bombing they were nearly worthless to either country. The Korean countryside was a much more ideal setting for the movement of the Communist Chinese light infantry than for the heavy, often road-bound, forces of the United States and its allies.

Sticking out into the Sea of Japan, Korea is a small country. It contains about the same land area as the state of Kansas. On a colored map, Korea looks like a sick appendix. Korea's value as the historical crossroads of Asia–"the sweet under-belly of China," as Charles Hemingway has called it–that declined with the spread of imperialist control and, to some degree, with the emergence of fairly modern transportation and communication methods. Divided down the middle by mountains and enduring extremes of temperature, hard rain, and deep snow, it had a culture both unique and imposed. Mountains cover more than 72 percent of the peninsula, with Mount Paektru the highest peak. In the words of one foot soldier, the terrain was "just one damn hill after the other." Surrounded by 3,579 islands, with a coastline of nearly 5,400 miles, and with a hostile borders, Korea was primarily an island. Yet, tidal variations, rapid rivers , and a jagged and difficult coastline it has few ports available for trade.

Even in the complex politic of the building Cold War, Korea was not in the late 1940s of much significance. Most members of the Truman administration, including the departments of State and Defense, believed that the best interests of the United States would be served by abandoning the government and people to whatever fate had in store for them. America had no sympathy with North Korea, which we saw as a part of the communist effort. Communists were the enemy. The military was not impressed by the prospect of involvement in South Korea and saw no military advantage to be gained from stationing troops there. The security of Japan did not count on the occupation of Korea, and given the other available locations, there was little value in even maintaining bases there.

When the time came, the United States would have been more than willing to pull out. When the Soviets began pushing on the Asian front, the United States used Korea for its own political gain. George Kennan, a longtime Soviet affairs advisor and director of the planning staff at the Department of State at the time, stated that the country should be looking to "get the best bargain" possible in Korea. In pursuance of this policy, the Truman administration recommended a United Nations election and the withdrawal of occupation troops. The United States was aware that the Soviet Union would never agree to a nationwide election; when as it blocked a nationwide election, the United States and UN settled for a South Korean election. An election was set up, a constitution was written, and Syngman Rhee was elected president. The United

States, as expected, offered limited economic or military aid.

The American attitude toward Korea was refined in National Security Document # 8 (1948). It indicated a willingness to provide aid but reaffirmed, as far as the United States was concerned, that South Korean government was totally responsible for protecting itself from the Communists. Troop withdrawal was affirmed by NSC # 8A, in early 1949. President Rhee pled for a pledge of support, but none was given.

The aid provided by Congress, in the light of these promises ,was nothing compared to what Rhee had wanted and requested, or to what was needed. The Congress believed that the security of South Korea could be maintained by a small, efficient, and well-trained force, and that the United States should not. take upon itself the economic burden of a large offensive military force. Nor did the Truman administration think South Korea should have too powerful a military force. There was some legitimate concern that President Rhee would use whatever military tools America provided him in aggressive action against North Korea.

Among the many contingency plans discussed by both the military and the Department of State, the primary one was that should the Democratic People's Republic of Korea attack the Republic of South Korea, the United States would withdraw its nationals from danger, then turn to the United Nations to consider what action should be taken. In terms of its own defense, the United States was well positioned in Asia, with bases in the Philippines, Okinawa, and Japan.

The geographical or military value of Korea in the eyes of the Truman administration increased when it appeared the Soviets were interested. With the outbreak of war, American expectations changed. America's first effort was defensive. After its success at Inchon, the American desires became more ambitious. After the entry of the Chinese Communists they became defensive again. The first goals, quickly established after the success at Inchon, were to defeat the Communists and free all of Korea. As the aggressive efforts failed and the war wound down, the American goals changed; holding on became the primary need. Eventually the United States was looking for little more than an honorable retreat and a military stalemate.

The timing of the war was poor, though certainly the United States did not choose the moment of invasion. What the United States did, however, was to assume this was the time to take a stand. That was understood by those involved in the decision. Most felt, however, that it was not the time to take on the Soviet Union in a war that would be, in a more contemporary phrase, the mother of all wars. The decision to act at this particular time was interesting but not necessarily prudent. Certainly the United States was not in the position militarily to support the aggressive actions that it took. Michael Pearlman, professor at the Command and Staff College in Fort Leavenworth, suggests the United States responded in Korea when it did was because "America could intervene in Korea, northeast Asia being one of the few places where the U.S. is capable of conducting immediate general offensive operations with its armed forces" [1998:12]. But it was not ready, and from the beginning the military would complain that the war in Korea restricted the extent of men and equipment that could be sent to NATO.

\Whether it was good timing in the long view the Cold War may be a different story. President Truman felt it was time to act, take a stand, and show Joseph Stalin and the Communists that America was willing to fight to prevent the expansion of their evil doctrine. Many, of course, assume that the primary enemy in the war was the Soviet Union. One suspects that General Bradley was really thinking of the Soviet Union when he called China "the wrong enemy."

Interestingly, some people do not seem to remember who it was that the United States fought in Korea. In a recent limited and off-the-cuff survey taken at several middle schools in Kansas City, Missouri, it became clear that the students did not know. The most consistent answer was that the United States fought the Russians. The primary enemy, however, was Red China.

\America entered the Korean War on the side of the United Nations and/or the Republic of South Korea. Within six months it was fighting the Communist Chinese. While the Chinese role increased, and in some military respects they directed the war, North Korea was always involved. Many seem to believe that once the Chinese entered the war, North Korea withdrew its forces or stopped fighting. On the other hand ,there were fewer Russian troops involved than many believe–probably no more than the few who had remained behind as military advisors. There were more Russian pilots, most likely, but no foot soldiers. The degree to which the Soviets were involved in strategic planning is hard to determine. Certainly Soviet tactics were employed, and much of the heavy equipment the North Koreans had was accompanied by engineers and tacticians from Russia.

The involvement of the Soviet Union is generally seen as being instrumental rather than direct. Even early in the historical analysis of the war it was believed that North Korea would not have acted without Soviet knowledge.

Later, Americans learned that its government had allowed United States pilots to fight in direct confrontations with Soviet pilots. The military knew, and Truman's administration certainly knew, but had chosen to keep it secret from the American people. It appears that more than sixty-five thousand Soviets were operating from bases in Manchuria. In general, however, the enemy in Korea is defined simply as "Communists," a category easily identified and widely hated.

Any deeper understanding of the situation must acknowledge that communism was not then, nor was it ever, a monolithic view. Nor was international communism, as we are inclined to identify the ideology, directed only from Moscow. The Soviet Union exerted a great deal of influence on its satellites, but "international communism" had many flavors, and some of them were far more nationalistic than international.

To hold the view that there was a single, well-directed, powerful Communist force with highly defined goals is to ignore the years of conflict within the Communist camp. This struggle is illustrated by the conflict between Russia and Vietnam, as well as China. Whether he intended to or not, President Truman played into the belief about a single-focus Communist effort when he told the American people that the attack on South Korea was all the evidence he needed. The Communists, he said, had passed beyond subversion to "conquer independent nations and will now use armed invasion and war."

Apparently believing this, and making the assumption that the attack on the Republic of South Korea was primarily an effort to draw attention away from events in Europe, Truman furthered America's commitment to the military defense of Europe. The force in Europe was increased from one to six infantry divisions, more than five hundred planes, and eighty-two warships. This meant that there were more troops defending our interests in Europe than fighting in Korea.

In what first appeared as a side issue but later proved important at this time—September 17, 1950, when United Nations troops were landing at Inchon—the Military Assistance Advisory Group (MAAG) was created in Vietnam. This unit, designed to provide closer working relations with South Vietnamese forces, would later become the Military Assistance Command Vietnam, in another war of major proportions.

There has been a revisionist tendency to focus historical inquiry more closely on local issues and the civil war as partial explanations for the Korean War. Bruce Cumings maintains that the war was not with North Korea or with Communist China, as such, but should be seen as a part of the collision between revolutionary nationalism in Asia and imperialism in America. Korea, and later Vietnam, were more than simply extensions of the Cold War divisions. William Stueck, in an excellent international book, urges historians to return to the international issues that emerged during the early months of the war. This discussion, as suggested above, has become more open since the dissolution of the Soviet Union [Stueck 1995]. There remains a great deal to be done on the validity of America's "anticommunist stand," both in Korea and Vietnam.

The question about China, and the predetermination of this communist state as our enemy, also must be considered. The lack of intelligence—and by that is meant the lack of prewar information and reasonable interpretations—had a great deal to do with both Chinese involvement and our surprise over it. While there is no doubt that Communist China became the major enemy, there were some surprising similarities between Chinese and American goals.

One of the interesting commonalities is that both were somewhat out of "synch" with what was happening. For both, compounding pressures that influenced most of their basic decisions were complex. They both lacked a clear picture of national identity, where they were going, and who was ford and against them. Both saw few other options than eventual war.

As the Korean War continued, both made an unsuccessful effort to "roll back" the degree of involvement, as well as investment, in it. At first, achieving their goals appeared, if not easy, certainly possible. Yet they found it harder and harder to do so. Many of the problems the United States dealt with seemed to arise from the fact that Americans were inclined to hold the Chinese military in contempt. They underestimated its size, its equipment, and in many respects, its intentions–an attitude reminiscent, some would say, of that of George Armstrong Custer at the Little Big Horn. GIs were wary of but not overawed at the possibility of dealing with the Chinese. Clay Blair quotes one man as expressing his contempt for the press attitude about the Chinese: "How many hordes in a platoon?" he asked. "I was attacked by two hordes and killed them both" [Blair, Clay 1987:645].

Both the United States and Communist China responded to what today we call the domino theory. Both were afraid of expansion of the war, and at the same time, both operated out of an unarticulated fear of subversive activities at home.

Looking at the differences, other than the ideological ones, the war aims of the United States appear to have been confused and unstable. During the war they moved from caution and pessimism to opportunism and anxiety. China seemed to have a much clearer perception of what was at stake. Nonetheless, Mao Tse tung, having established the basis for an armistice, signed the cease-fire without getting what he had asked for. He did not get the withdrawal of all United Nations forces from Korea, termination of American assistance to the Nationalist Chinese on Formosa, or assignment of Chiang Kai-shek's UN seat to Beijing–nor was he allowed to participate in the peace treaty that was signed with Japan.

There are some serious lessons to be learned from Korea. Paradoxically, one of the major lessons is that we do not seem to learn very well from history. We can sympathize with historian T. R. Fehrenbach, who has suggested that "having an imperfect sense of history, Americans sometimes forget as quickly as they learned."

Secretary of the Air Force Thomas K. Kinletter rationalized the events in Korea as a unique "never-to-be-repeated diversion from the true course of strategic air power." Lt. Gen. Maxwell D. Taylor, Eighth Army commander and later chairman of the Joint Chiefs of Staff during the Vietnam War, took another approach, suggesting that no analysis of mistakes in Korea was ever made and thus most of the mistakes were repeated [Summers, Harry 1996:1].

The war in Korea was a long, cruel, and bloody one. America was not ready for the war; its soldiers were not equal to the standards established in World War II. Gen. Matthew Ridgway was less than enthusiastic about the ability of his troops or of their leadership which consisted of "too many overage colonels and brigadiers, some of whom had failed at command during World War II" [Rose, Lisle 1999:253].

The soldiers, mainly occupation troops, were "soft, spoiled, and often poorly led." The marines, though nearly dissolved by President Truman and budget cuts, proved to be professional. The air force, particularly at the beginning, lived the interesting, and highly emotional, life of relaxing at home between flights dealing death and destruction.

The Korean War did provide a useful, even pragmatic, model, one that was eventually used in the Persian Gulf War. The Korean war was fought with conventional (not nuclear) weapons, a limited war in terms both of anticipated success and deployment, and of a primary (and primarily political) goal.

The difficulty of maintaining morale in the face of defeat and retreat was overcome, in some respects, by the professionalism of the military, especially the marines, who made advancing costly to the Chinese. It was the marines who claimed, while retreating in the face of the Chinese advance from the Chosin, "We are just advancing in the opposite direction." There is also the famous, if probably apocryphal, quote from Col. Lewis "Chesty" Puller: "The enemy is in front of us, behind us, to the left of us, and to the right of us. The bastards won't escape this time."

For years now, the armies of two conflicting ideologies have kept watch over the demilitarized zone, a stretch of land 2.5 miles wide running 155 miles across the peninsula. The situation today is no clearer, or any closer to unification, than when the war began. After many years, and in conjunction with political difficulties and military rumblings with North Korea, President Bill Clinton, in 1998, reaffirmed the value of the Korean Peninsula to American goals. An American presence remains.

Bibliography

Acheson, Dean. *Present at the Creation: My Years in the State Department.* New York: Norton, 1969.

Alexander, Joseph H., and Merrill L. Bartlett. *Sea Soldiers in the Cold War: Amphibious Warfare 1945-1991.* Annapolis, Md.: Naval Institute Press, 1995.

Ansel, Raymond B. *From Segregation to Desegregation: Blacks in the Army 1703-1994.* Carlisle Barracks, Pa.: U.S. Army War College, 1990.

Appleman, Roy E. *The United States Army in the Korean War: South to the Naktong, North to the Yalu.* Washington, D.C.: Office of the Chief of Military History, Department of the Army, 1987.

Archibald, Roger T. "History Is Not a Museum." *History News* 49 no.3 (May-June 1994): 11.

Ashley, David. *The Post Modern Condition.* Boulder Colo.: Westview Press, 1997.

Bacahus, William A. "The Relationship between Combat and Peace Negotiations: Fighting While Talking in Korea, 1951-1953." *Orbis (1962):* 545.

Berebitsky, William. *A Very Long Weekend: The Army National Guard In Korea 1950-1953.* Shippensburg, Pa.: White Mane, 1996.Bernstein, Barton J., ed. Politics and Policies of the Truman Administration. Chicago: Quadrangle, 1970.

Biskind, Peter. *Seeing Is Believing: How Hollywood Taught Us to Stop Worrying and Love the Fifties.* New York: Pantheon Books, 1983.

Blair, Clay. *The Forgotten War: America in Korea, 1950-1953.* New York: Times Books, 1987.

Bland, Larry I. ed. *The Papers of George C. Marshall.* 4 vols. Baltimore: Johns Hopkins Univ. Press, 1991.

Bodnar, John. *Remaking America: Public Memory, Commemoration, and Patriotism in the Twentieth Century.* Princeton, N. J.: Princeton Univ. Press, 1996.

Braun, Irwin , and Robert McCullough. "Reviewing the History Textbooks on the Korean War." *Graybeards* (August 1998): 47-48.

Breuer, William B. *Shadow Warriors: The Covert War in Korea.* New York: Wiley, 1996.

Brune, Lester H. *The Korean War: Handbook of the Literature and Research*
    Westport, Conn.: Greenwood Press, 1996.
Cagle, Malcolm W., and Frank A. Manson. *The Sea War in Korea.* Annapolis, Md.:
    U. S. Naval Institute, 1957.
Chace, James. *Acheson: The Secretary of State Who Created the American World*
    New York: Simon and Schuster, 1998.
Clark, Ian. *Waging War.* Oxford: Clarendon Press, 1990.
Collins, J. Lawton. *War in Peacetime: The History and Lessons of Korea.* Boston:
    Houghton Mifflin, 1969.
Cotton, James, and Ian Neary, eds. *The Korean War in History.* Manchester, U.K.:
    Manchester Univ. Press, 1989.
Cumings, Bruce. *Korea's Place in the Sun: A Modern History.* New York: W.
    W.Norton, 1997.
Cumings, Bruce. "'Revising Postrevisionism,' or The Poverty of Theory in American
    Diplomatic History." *Diplomatic History* 17 (Fall 1993): 539-569.
Cumings, Bruce. *The Roaring of the Cataract, 1947-1950* 2 vols. Princeton, N. J.:
    Princeton Univ. Press, 1981, 1990.
Cumings, Bruce. *War and Television.* London: Verso, 1992.
Cumings, Bruce, and Jon Halliday. *The Unknown War: Korea.* New York:
    Pantheon,1988.
DeWeerd, H. A. "Strategic Surprise in the Korean War." *Orbis* (1962): 435-452.
Diggins, John R. *The Proud Decade: America in War and in Peace, 1941-1960.* New
    York: Norton, 1988.
Dillie, John. *Substitute for Victory.* New York: Doubleday, 1954.
Dingman, Roger. "Truman, Attlee and the Korean War Crisis." In *The East Asian
    Crisis,1945-1951, The Problem of China, Korea, and Japan: Papers.* London:
    International Center for Economics, and Related Disciplines: London School of
    Economics, 1982.
Dingman, Roger. "Atomic Diplomacy During the Korean War." *International Security*
    13 (Winter 1998-1989): 61-89.
Dockrill, Michael, and John Young, eds. *British Foreign Policy, 1945-1956.*London:
    Macmillan, 1989:16-148
Dong-A, Ilbo. *Basic Documents on Security and Unification.* Seoul: Dong-A, 1971.
Drought, James. *The Secret.* Norwalk: Skylight Press, 1963.
Ebbert, Jean, and Marie-Beth Hall. *Cross Currents: Navy Women from WWI to
    Tailhook.* Washington, D.C.: Brassey's, 1993.
Edwards, Paul M. *General Matthew B. Ridgway: A Bibliography.* Westport, Conn.:
    Greenwood Press, 1993.
Edwards, Paul M.*The Korean War: An Annotated Bibliography.* Westport, Conn.:
    Greenwood Press, 1998.
Eisenhower, Dwight D. *Mandate for Change.* Garden City, N.Y.: Doubleday, 1963.
Endicott, Stephen, and Edward Hagerman. *The United States and Biological Warfare:
    Secrets from the Early Cold War and Korea.* Bloomington: Univ. of Indiana Press,
    1998.
Evanhoe, Ed. *Darkmoon: Eighth Army Special Operations in the Korean War.*
    Annapolis, Md.: Naval Institute Press, 1995.
Fehrenbach, T. R. *This Kind of War: A Study in Unpreparedness.* New York:
    Macmillan,1963.

Macmillan,1963.

Feis, Herbert. *From Trust to Terror: The Onset of the Cold War, 1945-1950.* New York: Norton, 1970.

Field, James A. Jr. *History of the United States Naval Operations: Korea* Washington, D.C.: Government Printing Office, 1962.

Foot, Rosemary. "Making Known the Unknown War: Policy Analysis of The Korean Conflict in the Last Decade."*Diplomatic History* 15 no. 3 (Summer 1991)" 411-431.

Foot, Rosemary. *A Substitute for Victory: The Politics of Peacemaking and the Korean Armistice Talks.* Ithaca, N. Y.: Cornell Univ. Press, 1990.

Foot, Rosemary."Nuclear Coercion and the Ending of the Korean Conflict."*International Security* 13 (Winter 1988-1989): 99-112.

Foot, Rosemary. *The Wrong War: American Policy and the Dimensions of the Korean Conflict, 1950-1953.* Ithaca, N. Y.: Cornell Univ. Press, 1985.

Friedman, Edward, and Mark Selden. *American Asia: Dissenting Essays on Asian-American Relations.* New York: Pantheon, 1971.

Futrell, Robert F. *The United States Air Force in Korea, 1950-1953.* New York: Duell, Sloan and Pearce, 1983.

Gardner, Lloyd C. *The Korean War.* New York: Quadrangle, 1972

Goldstein, Warren. "Editorial," *The Chronicle of Higher Education* (April 10, 1998): A64.

Goodman, Allen E., ed. *Negotiating While Fighting: The Diary of Admiral C. Turner Joy at the Korean Armistice Conference.* Stanford, Calif.: Hoover Institution Press, 1978.

Goulden, Joseph C. *Korea: The Untold Story of the War.* New York: Times Books, 1982.

Greenfield, Meg. "Missing World War II." *Newsweek* , June 6, 1994, 86.

Grey, Jeffrey. *The Commonwealth Armies and the Korean War: An Alliance Study* New York: Manchester Univ. Press, 1988.

Gupta, Karunakar. "How Did the Civil War Begin?" *China Quarterly 52,* 1972: 699-716.

Gurtov, Melvin, and Byong Moo Hwang. *China under Threat.* Baltimore: Johns Hopkins Press, 1960.

Guttman, Allen. *Korea and the Theory of Limited War.* Boston: D. C. Heath, 1967.

Hagiwara, Ryo *The Korean Wqar: The Conspiracies by Kim Il Sung and MacArthur* Typed manuscript located at the Center for the Study of the Korean War, np,nd.

Halberstam, David. *The Fifties.* New York: Villard, 1993.

Halliday, Jon. "Air Operations in Korea: The Soviet Side of the Story." In *A Revolutionary War: Korea and the Transformation of the Postwar World,* ed. William J. Williams. Chicago: Imprint Publications, 1993.

Halliday, Jon. "The Korean War: Some Notes on Evidence and Solidarity." *Bulletin of Concerned Asian Scholars* 3 (November 1979): 2-18.

Halliday, Jon, and Bruce Cumings. *The Unknown War: Korea.* New York: Pantheon Books, 1998.

Hallion, Richard P. "Naval Air Operations in Korea." In *A Revolutionary War: Korea and the Transformation of the Postwar World,* ed. William J. Williams. Chicago: Imprint Publications, 1993.

Hallion, Richard P. *The Naval Air War in Korea.* Baltimore: Nautical and Aviation, 1986.

Hammel, Eric M. *Chosin: Heroic Ordeal of the Korean War.* New York: Vanguard Press, 1981.

Hastings, Max. *The Korean War.* New York: Simon and Schuster, 1987.

Hankuk, Jon Jang Sa *History of the Korean War.* 5 vol. Seoul: Hangrim, 1990, 1992. J. Glen Grey. New York, 1968.

Heinl, Robert D., Jr. *Victory at High Tide: The Inchon-Seoul Campaign.* New York:

Heidegger, Martin. *What Is Called Thinking.* Trans J. B. Lippincott. Harper. Chicago: Harper and Row,1968.

Hermes, Walter. *Truce Tent and Fighting Front: United States in the Korean War.* Washington, D.C.: Center of Military History, 1966, 1991.

Higgins, Marguerite. *War in Korea: The Report of a Woman Combat Correspondent.* Garden City, N. Y.: Doubleday, 1951.

Hoyt, Edwin P. *The Bloody Road to Panmunjom.* New York: Stein & Day, 1985.

Hunt, Michael H. "Beijing and the Korean Crisis, June 1950-June 1951." *Political Science Quarterly* 107, no. 3 (1992): 477.

Huston, James A. *Guns and Butter, Powder and Rice: U. S. Army Logistics of the Korean War.* Selinsgrove, Pa.: Susquehanna Univ. Press, 1989.

Ikle, Fred C. *Every War Must End.* New York: Columbia Univ. Press, 1991.

Jackson, Robert. *Air War over Korea.* New York: Scribner's, 1973.

James, D. Clayton. *The Years of MacArthur: Triumph and Disaster, 1945-1964.* Vol 3. Boston: Houghton - Mifflin, 1985.

James, D. Clayton, and Anne S. Wells. *Refighting the Last War: Command and Crisis in Korea, 1950-1953.* New York: Free Press, 1993.

Jin, Chul Soh. "Some Causes of the Korean War of 1950: A Study of Foreign Involvement in Korea (1945-1950). Ph.D diss.,Univ. of Oklahoma. 1963.

Kaufman, Burton I. The Korean War: Challenges in Crisis, Credibility, and Command. Pa.: Temple Univ. Press. 1986.

Kemp, Robert F. *Combined Operations in the Korean War.* Carlisle Barracks, Pa.: U. S. Army War College, 1989.

Kennan, George F. *Memories 1925-1950 and 1950-1963.* Boston: Atlantic, Little Brown, 1967, 1972.

Kerin, James, Jr. "The Korean War and American Memory." Ph. D. diss., University of Pennsylvania, 1994.

Knox, Donald. *The Korean War: Uncertain Victory.* San Diego: Harcourt Brace Jovanovich, 1988.

Kolko, Gabriel, and Joyce Kolko. *The Limits of Power: The World and the United States Foreign Policy, 1945-1954.* New York: Harper, 1972.

LaFeber, William. *America, Russia and the Cold War, 1945-1975.* New York: Wiley, 1967.

Landsdown, John R. P. *With the Carriers in Korea: The Sea and Air War in SE Asia 1950-1953.* Wilmslow, Cheshire, U.K.: Crecy, 1997.

Leckey, Thomas. "Teaching History at High Noon: Letting the Lessons Emerge." *Commonweal* 118, (April 5, 1991, 22.

Leckie, Robert. *Conflict: The History of the Korean War.* New York: Da Capo, 1962,1996.

Leckie, Robert. *The March to Glory.* Cleveland: World, 1960.

Leffler, Melvyn P. *A Preponderance of Power: National Security, The Truman Administration, and the Cold War.* Stanford, Calif.: Stanford Univ. Press, 1992.

Levine, Steven I. "Soviet-American Rivalry in Manchuria and the Cold War." In *Dimensions of China's Foreign Relations,* ed. Hsueh Chun-tu. New York: Praeger, 1977:10-43.

Lewis, John W., Sergei N. Goncharov, and Litai Xue. *Uncertain Partners: Stalin, Mao, and the Korean War.* Stanford, Calif.: Stanford Univ. Press, 1993.

Lowe, Peter. "The Significance of the Korean War in Anglo-American Relations." In *British Foreign Policy, 1945-1956,* ed. Michael Dockrill and John W. Young. London: Macmillan, 1989.

MacArthur, Douglas. *Reminiscences.* New York: Da Capo, 1964.

MacDonald, Callum. "Rediscovering History: New Light on the Unknown War: Korea." *Bulletin of Concerned Asian Scholars* 244 (October 1992): 62.

Marshall, S. L.A. *Pork Chop Hill.* New York: Jove Press, 1986.

Marshall, S.L.A. *The River and the Gauntlet: Defeat of the Eighth Army by the Communist Chinese Forces, November 1950.* New York: Morrow, 1953.

Matray, James L. *Historical Dictionary of the Korean War.* Westport, Connecticut: Greenwood Press, 1991.

Matray, James I. *The Reluctant Crusade: American Foreign Policy in Korea 1941-1950.* Honolulu: University of Hawaii Press, 1985.

Merrill, John. *Korea: The Peninsular Origins of the War.* Newark: Univ. of Delaware Press, 1989.

Meyers, Edward. *Thunder in the Morning Calm: The Royal Navy in Korea, 1950-1955.* St. Catharines, Ont.: Vanwell, 1991.

Millett, Allen. *Semper Fidelis: The History of the United States Marine Corps.* New York: Free Press, 1980, 1991.

Moeller, Susan D. *Shooting War: Photography and the American Combat Experience.* New York: Basic Books, 1991.

Montross, Lynn. *United States Marine Operation in Korea 1950-1953.* 5 vol. Washington, D. C.: Historical Branch, G-3, Headquarters, U.S. Marine Corps, 1954-1972.

Morton, Lois. "Willoughby on MacArthur: Myth and Reality." *Reporter* 11, November 4, 1956. 46.

Mossman, Billy C. *Ebb and Flow, November 1950-July 1951: TheUnited States in the Korean War.* Washington, D.C.: Center of Military History, 1990.

Mueller, John E. *War, Presidents and Public Opinion.* New York: John Wiley & Sons, 1973.

Neal, Arthur G. *National Trauma and Collective Memory.* London: M. E. Sharpe, 1998.

Niebuhr, Reinhold. *The Irony of American History.* New York: Scribner's, 1952.

Nietzsche, Friedrich. *The Gay Science,* Trans. Walter Kaufmann.. New York: Penguin Book, Inc.,1974.

Oliver, Robert T. *Why War Came to Korea.* New York: Fordham Univ.Press, 1950.

Paschall, Rod. *A Study in Command and Control: Special Operations in Korea, 1951-1953.* Carlisle Barracks, Pa.: U. S. Army Military History Institute, 1988.

Pearlman, Michael. "Korea: Fighting a War While Fearing to Fight One, the Specter of Escalation Management." Unpublished manuscript held by author.

Piehler, Guenter Kurt. *Remembering the War the American Way: 1783 to the Present.* Washington, D.C.: Smithsonian Institution, 1995.

Purden, Wesley. "The New History Breeds Dunces." *Insight* (May 25, 1992): 17.

Rose, Lisle A. *The Cold War Comes to Main Street: America in 1950.* Lawrence: Univ. of Kansas Press. 1999.

Ruetten, Richard T. "General Douglas MacArthur's 'Reconnaissance in Force': The Rationalization of Defeat in Korea." *Pacific Historical Review* 36 (February 1967): 87.

Ryan, Mark A. *Chinese Attitudes toward Nuclear Weapons: China and the United States during the Korean War.* London: East Gate Book, 1989.

Sandler, Stanley, ed. *The Korean War: An Encyclopedia.* New York: Garland, 1995.

Schaller, Michael. *Douglas MacArthur: The Far East General.* New York: Oxford Univ. Press, 1989.

Schnabel, James F. *Policy and Direction: The First Year.* Washington, D.C.: Department of the Army, 1972.

Schnabel, James F., and Robert J. Watson. *The Korean War.* Washington, D. C.: Joint Chiefs of Staff, 1978. Washington D.C.: Joint Chiefs of Staff, 1978.

"Secrets of the Korean War." *U.S. News and World Report,* August 9, 1993.

Severo, Richard, and Lewis Milford. *The Wages of War: When Americans Came Home: From Valley Forge to Vietnam.* New York: Simon and Schuster, 1997.

Serwood, John D. *Officers in Flight Suits: The Story of American Air Force Pilots in the Korean War.* New York: New York Univ. Press, 1996.

Sheldon, Walt. *Hell or High Water: MacArthur's Landing at Inchon.* New York: Macmillan, 1968.

Simmons, Robert. *The Strained Alliance: Peking, Pyongyang, Moscow and the Politics of the Cold War.* New York: Free Press, 1975.

Soderbergh, Peter A. *Women Marines in the Korean War Era.* Westport, Conn.: Praeger, 1994.

Soffer, Joanthan M. *General Matthew R. Ridgway: From Progressivism to Reaganism, 1895-1993.* Westport, Conn.: Praeger, 1998.

Son-Yup, Paik. *From Pusan to Panmunjom.* Washington, D.C. Brassey's, 1992.

Spanier, John W. *The Truman-MacArthur Controversy and the Korean War.* New York: W. W. Norton 1965.

Stairs, Denis. *The Diplomacy of Constraint: Canada, the Korean War, and the United States.* Toronto: Univ. of Toronto Press, 1974.

Stanton, Shelby L. *America's Tenth Legion: X Corps in Korea, 1950.* Novato, Calif.: Presidio Press, 1989.

Stearn, Peter N. *Meaning over Memory.* Chapel Hill: University of North Carolina, 1993.

Stephanson, Anders. *Kennan and the Art of Foreign Policy.* Cambridge, Mass.: Harvard Univ. Press, 1995.

Stockholm International Peace Research Institute. *The Problem of Chemical and Biological Warfare.* 6 volumes. New York: Stockholm International Peace Research Institute, 1956.

Stone, I. F. *Hidden History of the Korean War.* Boston: Little Brown, 1952.

Stueck, William. *The Korean War: An International History.* Princeton:, N. J.: Princeton Univ. Press, 1995.

Su Guang, Zhang. *Mao's Military Romanticism: China and the Korean War, 1950–1953.* Lawrence: Univ. of Kansas Press. 1995.

Summers, Harry G., Jr. "The Korean War: A Fresh Perspective." *Military History* (April 1996): 1-8.

Swartout, Robert Jr. "American Historians and the Outbreak of the Korean War: An Historiographical Essay." *Asian Quarterly* [Belgium] no. 11, 1979, 67-77.

Taylor, Maxwell D. *The Uncertain Trumpet.* New York: Harper, 1960.

Toland, John. *In Mortal Combat.* New York: William Morrow, 1991.

Voorhees, Melvin B. *Korean Tales.* New York: Simon and Schuster, 1952.

Weathersby, Kathryn. "Soviet Aims in Korea and the Origins of the Korean War, 1945-1950: New Evidence from the Russian Archives." Cold War International History Project Working Paper no. 8, November 1995.

West, Philip. "Interpreting the Korean War." *American Historical Review* 94 (February 1989): 80-96.

Whitney, Courtney. *MacArthur: His Rendezvous with History.* New York: Alfred A. Knopf, 1956.

Wilz, John Edward. "The MacArthur Hearings of 1951: The Secret Testimony." *Military Affairs* 39 (December 1975): 167.

Xi, Zhang. "China's Entry into the Korean War." *Chinese Historians* 6 (Spring 1993):1-30.

Yergin, Daniel. *Shattered Peace.* Boston: Houghton Mifflin, 1977.

Yibo, Bo. "The Making of the 'Lean-to-One-Side' Decision." Trans. Zhai Qiang. *Chinese Historians* 5 (Spring 1992): 57-62.

Yu, Bin. "What China Learned from Its 'Forgotten War' in Korea." *Strategic Review* (Summer 1998): 4-16.

Subject Index

Military Unit Index

About the Author

PAUL M. EDWARDS is Coordinator of Assessment and Evaluation for Baker University at Overland Park, Kansas. He is also the founder and Executive Director of the Center for the Study of the Korean War, an archival foundation located in Independence, Missouri. The author of several books on the Korean War, he teaches classes on the Korean War at Baker and Park College.

ISBN 0-313-31021-1

9 780313 310218

90000>

HARDCOVER BAR CODE